Marcus's
France

Dad,

This book is for you. I know you would have loved it, as it brings back memories of those early days when we both began this journey.

Always in my thoughts,

Marcus

Marcus's France

Delicious French recipes, from my kitchen to yours

MARCUS WAREING

with Bridget Powell and Lisa Harrison

PHOTOGRAPHY BY MATT RUSSELL

HarperCollins*Publishers*

Introduction

My career as a chef has spanned almost 40 years and I can honestly say there's one cuisine which has influenced me far and above any other: the food of France. When I first went to catering college in 1986 my training was all about classic French recipes and techniques. There I learned the basics of filleting fish, portioning chicken, making sauces, gravies, pâtés, terrines and pastries, all in the time-honoured French style. Back then, and still today in many places, French cooking was considered the height of sophistication. Mastering the basics at college fuelled my desire to become the best I could be and launched my career as a chef.

And who could blame me? What's not to love about French food? Famously rich dishes packed with butter and cream like dauphinoise potatoes, moules marinière and clafoutis. Then there is the incredible patisserie: croissants, macarons and – my favourite – millefeuille. And some of the very best ingredients in the world: incomparable bread; delicious wines; and don't get me started on the cheese . . . The world of gastronomy owes a lot to France. It's no wonder to me that French food is so globally revered and that their recipes have stood the test of time.

After college I headed for London where I worked in some of the most acclaimed restaurants in the capital, first at The Savoy where I was one of 130 chefs in the kitchen. I was stationed in the cold fish section where I spent seven months (yes, seven!) filleting, shelling, picking and prepping fish and seafood. That was certainly an education! From there I landed a job at then three Michelin-starred Le Gavroche, the beacon of French cuisine in London. Run by the incredible Roux family, there was a year long waiting list to work there. But on the advice of my dad, I knocked on the door on my day off and simply asked for a job. The sous chef was from Wigan and must have seen a kindred spirit standing on the doorstep because he said yes; before I knew it, I was working for the elite. There was no bigger or better French kitchen in London at that time. It's also where I first met Gordon Ramsay (more on that in a moment).

After an amazing year at Le Gavroche, Albert Roux sent me to Upstate New York. It was 1991, the year I turned 21. No one stayed at Le Gavroche for more than 12 months, but Albert would always try to help his young chefs continue their training in other kitchens. Having decided he couldn't send me to France because I didn't speak the language, he shipped me off to America instead. Quite the result for a young lad! Albert set me up with a job at a resort in the Adirondack Mountains, just south of the border from the French-speaking region of Canada, and where he was the consultant chef. I took all my training and time spent working in London and brought my French style of cooking to this small hotel by the idyllic Saranac Lake. Here I learned how to master the outdoor grill and the art of cooking over fire. It's been a fantastic addition to my skill set and a way that I now cook more and more.

From there I spent a year in Amsterdam where I trained with two French bakers. I wanted to plug a gap in my knowledge and learn the art of classic French patisserie like croissants and pain au chocolat. And later, while working at Gravetye Manor in Sussex, I was lucky enough to meet the great Pierre Koffman; it's also where I met my incredible wife, Jane. Pierre invited me to come and work a stage (a brief and unpaid internship) in his restaurant La Tante Claire, which had three Michelin stars. Gordon was Pierre's sous chef and after one day working together, he told me to knock on his door if I ever wanted a full-time job, which is exactly what I did one week later. All this is to say that I have been lucky enough to meet, work with and train under some of the true icons of French cuisine, all of whom have influenced the way I cook today.

Soon after I started working for Gordon, he sent me to Paris. After all my training, I was finally cooking in France! I spent almost a year at Restaurant Guy Savoy, another three-star establishment. Gordon himself had trained there and knew it was exactly what I needed to reach the next level with my own cooking. I never really understood passion until I arrived in Paris. Spending time in France truly opened my eyes: the precision, the dedication, the respect for their craft and ingredients was everywhere from the fine dining restaurants to the boulangeries. I couldn't walk past a deli or patisserie without stopping to stare through the window and I used to live on millefeuille. Those were the days!

And that was it, my training was over. I came back to London in 1995 and, aged 25, opened my first restaurant with Gordon. I put into practice everything I'd learned, by now the food of France was truly ingrained in every fibre of my being as a chef. It was time to dig into my repertoire and create fine dining food in the French style that I'd grown to love. Six months later I was one of the youngest people ever to gain a Michelin star.

In this book I want to take you on a journey, my journey through the world of French food and the ways in which it has inspired me throughout my career. I want to share with you all those basic recipes I learned at college like Choux Pastry (see page 47), Confit de Canard (see page 39) and the ever-versatile roux sauce, which is responsible for some of the true culinary greats, including my Croque Madame (see page 20).

The classics I discovered at The Savoy, like Apple Tarte Tatin (see page 81) and Omelette Arnold Bennett (see page 57) and the memorable meals I've enjoyed while travelling through and working in France, like Tarte Flambée with Brie and Onion (see page 144) and Mushroom and Jerusalem Artichoke Velouté (see page 142). Then there are the many dishes I cook for my family, whether we're on a French holiday or at home, such as Pork Chops with Green Olive Sauce (see page 194), Bouillabaisse-inspired Fish Soup (see page 208) and Cherry Clafoutis (see page 226), all of which bring an unmistakable taste of France into our kitchen.

I'm not necessarily reinventing the wheel with these recipes, but I do want to inspire you to cook some of the great classics for yourself. They're classics for a reason and I've brought them up to date to suit our modern world and busy lives, using simpler techniques, a lighter touch and time-saving tips. We have access now to a wider range of fresher ingredients; we can eat pork and certain game cooked pink . . . times have changed. With this book I want to dig deep into the archive of French recipes I've loved over the years and give them a fresh new approach.

A NOTE ON INGREDIENTS

In this book I use large free-range eggs, unsalted butter, free-range chicken, whole milk (but semi-skimmed can be substituted) and medium-sized fruit and vegetables – unless the recipe states otherwise. Also, I use Maldon salt when cooking, unless a recipe requires a finer salt, then it's usually table salt.

A NOTE ON DESSERTS

When you think of French desserts, it's easy to feel intimidated. The complicated pastries, tarts and cakes you see in patisserie windows are so enticing, impressive and utterly delicious that it's hard to imagine making them at home with ease. But in this book, scattered throughout the different chapters, you'll find a huge variety of classic French desserts made simple, desserts

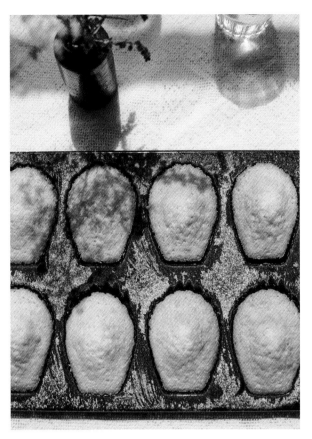

that are just as tasty and impressive as the ones you see in France. You just need to have a few tricks up your sleeve. For example, I never make my own puff pastry these days, shop-bought can be of such high quality and unlocks the door to so many otherwise complicated recipes. My only advice would be to opt for an all-butter puff pastry if you can. You'll also notice that I use tinned fruit in some of my recipes, or suggest it as an alternative to fresh. I love tinned fruit! It's picked and preserved when it's in season and gives you delicious-tasting and affordable produce at any time of the year. It's also easy to bake with so it's a no-brainer for me. When it comes to chocolate, the higher the cocoa content the better, certainly no less than 70%. I find dark chocolate gives a fabulously rich, fruity flavour to my desserts. With great ingredients and the right techniques, I believe anyone can make sweet treats worthy of a Parisian patisserie window.

FINALLY, SOME HEARTFELT THANKS

During my career I've been extremely lucky to take inspiration and to learn from some of the greatest chefs in the world; I wouldn't be the cook I am today without their guidance. Some are French and others are honorary Frenchmen in my eyes, all of whom I want to thank. Firstly, those who trained me: Anton Edelmann, Albert Roux, Michel Roux Jnr, Gordon Ramsay and Guy Savoy. Then the top chefs of the late eighties who provided early inspiration through their TV appearances and cookbooks while I was at college: Nico Ladenis, Anton Mosimann, Michel Roux Snr, Peter Kromberg, Michael Nadell, Richard Shepherd, Pierre Koffman, Marco Pierre White, Raymond Blanc. And lastly, the true icons of the industry whose legendary restaurants have been such an inspiration: Alain Ducasse, Roger Vergé, Paul Bocuse, Joël Robuchon, Michel Bras and George Blanc. Just writing these names brings back so many memories and I'm deeply grateful for the influence each and every one of them has had on my career.

Now, get cooking and enjoy your own journey through the incredible world of French food.

College

Days

Let me take you back to the September of 1986. I was living in Southport with my mum, dad, brother and sisters. Although my two passions in life were boxing and working with my dad, I had decided to leave the relative comfort of my father's fruit and potato warehouse and follow in my older brother's footsteps by enrolling in catering college. It was a magical time for me. I loved getting hands on in the kitchen and learning all the basic techniques. I would spend hours with my nose in cookbooks written by some of the greatest French chefs in the world, soaking up every morsel of information I could. I had truly found my calling in life. These days I find that no matter what I make, whether it's an overtly French recipe like beef bourguignon or a simple barbecue dish like a whole cooked sea bream, it's still those basic techniques and grounding in French cookery that I apply to all my recipes.

In this chapter I want to share some of those techniques and recipes with you. These are the recipes that – I think – will help to build an incredible foundation in the French style of cooking, but I also hope to empower you to use them in different ways. For example, you'll find a recipe for hollandaise sauce and a way I like to use it with hazelnut crusted fish, but the possibilities for hollandaise are endless; once you've mastered the sauce itself you can let your imagination run wild. I hope you find that's the case for a lot of the recipes in this chapter.

Croque Madame

Sirloin Steak with Piquant Brandy Sauce

Pan-fried Fish with Crushed
New Potatoes and Sauce Grenobloise

Chicken Supreme with Mushroom Cream Sauce

White Fish with Hazelnut Crumb
and Hollandaise Sauce

Compound Butters

Chicken Liver Parfait

Pork and Pheasant Terrine

Confit de Canard

Tournedos Rossini

Quiche Lorraine

Mushroom Duxelles

Churros with Lavender Sugar and Citrus Cream

St Clements Citrus Tart

Croque Madame

A classic roux sauce is the foundation for so many great recipes and although I didn't learn about it until I went to college, it's one of the first things my wife Jane taught our kids to make when they were young. It opens so many culinary doors: macaroni cheese, lasagne, moussaka and arguably the best sandwiches in France – croques monsieur and madame. Layers of cheese, ham and luxurious roux sauce sandwiched between two slices of bread, toasted in butter and – in the case of the croque madame – topped with a perfectly fried egg. Sandwiches may have been invented in Great Britain, but the French really took them to a whole new level with this fabulous recipe.

SERVES: 2
PREP TIME: UNDER 10 MINUTES
COOKING TIME: ABOUT 20 MINUTES

100g Gruyère cheese, grated

4 slices of sourdough

4 slices of prosciutto

1 tbsp butter

olive oil, for frying

2 eggs

watercress or lamb's lettuce, to serve

FOR THE ROUX SAUCE
200ml milk

2 tsp fresh thyme leaves

2 tbsp butter

2 tbsp plain flour

1 tsp Dijon mustard

2 tsp wholegrain mustard

100g Cheddar cheese, grated

sea salt and freshly
ground black pepper

1. Start by making the roux sauce. Put the milk and thyme into a small saucepan. Gently bring to a simmer over low heat. Melt the butter in another small saucepan, then add the flour and a pinch each of salt and pepper. Cook over low heat for about 1 minute to get rid of the floury taste but avoid letting it brown. Gradually whisk in half of the hot milk, then add the remaining milk and cook for a further 5 minutes over low heat, stirring continuously. Remove from the heat, add the mustards and cheese and stir until the cheese has melted.

2. Preheat the oven to 200°C/180°C fan/gas 6 and line a baking tray with baking parchment.

3. Divide the grated Gruyère between two slices of the sourdough, then top with the prosciutto. Finish with two-thirds of the roux sauce then top with the other slices of sourdough. Spread the remaining roux sauce on top. Heat a large frying pan over medium heat. When hot, add the butter then carefully add the sandwiches and toast them for 3–5 minutes. Gently turn the sandwiches over and brown the other side for another 3–5 minutes.

4. Transfer to the lined baking tray and bake in the oven for 4–5 minutes until the cheese has melted.

5. While the sandwiches are baking, heat a little olive oil in a frying pan and crack both eggs into the pan. Fry for 2–3 minutes, or until the white is set and the yolk is still soft.

6. Place the sandwiches on two separate plates and top each with a fried egg. Serve with watercress or lamb's lettuce on the side.

Sirloin Steak with Piquant Brandy Sauce

A piquant sauce is sharp and tangy, but in the most delicious way. In this case, the sharpness comes from the addition of capers and gherkins to this classic creamy brandy sauce. This is another great bedrock recipe and I definitely recommend you having this in your repertoire. Once you've mastered it, you'll see that you can easily swap out the gherkins and capers for peppercorns or mushrooms to give you even more classic sauces to accompany steak. Photographed overleaf.

SERVES: 2
PREP TIME: 15 MINUTES
COOKING TIME: 25–35 MINUTES

1 tbsp olive oil

2 × 200–250g sirloin steaks

40g butter, cubed

2 garlic cloves, bashed

4 sprigs of fresh thyme

sea salt and freshly
ground black pepper

FOR THE PIQUANT BRANDY SAUCE

4 shallots, thinly sliced

2 small garlic cloves, finely grated

4 tbsp brandy

100ml good-quality beef stock

2 tbsp capers, drained

1 gherkin, finely chopped

2 tbsp crème fraîche

small handful of fresh tarragon,
leaves picked and finely chopped

1. Heat the oil in a heavy-based frying pan (one that will comfortably fit both steaks) over high heat. When smoking, season the steaks on one side with salt and pepper and carefully place them seasoned side down in the pan. Give the pan a gentle shake to ensure there is oil under the steaks. Fry for about 2 minutes until nicely browned on one side, then season the second side with salt and pepper and carefully turn over and brown for another 2 minutes.

2. Flip the steaks back to the original side and add the butter, cube by cube, the garlic and two of the thyme sprigs to the pan. When the butter starts to foam, tilt the pan towards you and spoon it over the steaks. After 1 minute of basting, turn the steaks over and baste the other sides for a further minute.

3. Remove them from the pan at this point if you like them more on the rare to medium-rare side, or if you prefer them cooked further, turn the heat down a little and continue to baste for a further 3–4 minutes (the cooking time will depend on the thickness of the steak, and the doneness you prefer). When you remove the steaks from the pan, keep them somewhere warm and cover with another plate or foil to rest.

4. Strain the contents of the pan through a fine sieve, discarding the garlic and thyme. Clean the pan and place back over medium heat with the strained pan juices, ready to make the sauce.

5. When the pan juices are hot, add the shallots, grated garlic, remaining thyme sprigs and a generous grind of black pepper. Cook for about 4 minutes until the shallots are soft, then add the brandy and cook for a further 3 minutes. Add the beef stock and simmer for 3 minutes, remove the pan from the heat and pick out the thyme stalks. Add the drained capers and gherkin and stir through the crème fraîche.

6. Scatter over the tarragon and taste the sauce, adding more salt and pepper if needed.

7. Your steaks will be well rested at this point. Place on warm plates and pour the sauce over the steaks.

MARCUS'S TIP

Only ever season steak right before you cook it, otherwise the salt can draw out the moisture that you want to keep inside the meat. Season the first side right before you put it in the pan, seasoned side down, then wait until you're about to turn it over before seasoning the second side.

Pan-fried Fish with Crushed New Potatoes and Sauce Grenobloise

Sauce Grenobloise is perhaps one of the lesser-known sauces of France, but it's definitely one of my favourites and one that I learned to make at college. Hailing from the city of Grenoble at the foot of the Alps in southeast France, it's said to have been invented there as a means of making fish that was past its best – due to the landlocked location of the city – taste amazing. Packed with zingy flavours and not too dissimilar to another French classic, meunière, its base is a nutty brown butter. It pairs perfectly with all sorts of fish and seafood – I particularly love it with salmon or any firm white fish.

SERVES: 4
PREP TIME: 10 MINUTES
COOKING TIME: 20–30 MINUTES

FOR THE SAUCE GRENOBLOISE

2 slices of white bread, crusts removed

100g butter

50g capers

1 lemon, peel and pith removed, and cut into segments

small handful of fresh flat-leaf parsley, chopped

FOR THE FISH

4 x 120g cod, haddock or sea bass fillet portions, skin on

olive oil

sea salt and freshly ground black pepper

FOR THE POTATOES

600g new potatoes
20g butter

TO SERVE

lemon wedges

1. First prepare the croutons. Lightly roll the bread slices with a rolling pin to flatten, then cut into 1cm dice and set aside.

2. To make the sauce, melt the butter in a frying pan over medium heat and cook for 2–3 minutes until foaming and beginning to turn a nut-brown colour. Add the diced bread and cook for 3–4 minutes until crisp and golden brown. Remove from the heat and stir through the capers, segmented lemon and parsley, then season to taste with salt (bear in mind that the brine from the capers is slightly salty).

3. Cook the new potatoes in a saucepan of boiling salted water for 10–15 minutes, or until tender. Drain and crush lightly with a fork, then add the butter, season with salt and pepper and set aside.

4. Heat a frying pan until hot. Drizzle the fish with a little olive oil, season with salt and pepper and then fry skin side down for 3–4 minutes, or until the skin is golden. Flip over and cook for another 2 minutes on the other side, or until the fish is just cooked through.

5. Serve the pan-fried fish with the sauce spooned over, the crushed potatoes on the side and lemon wedges for squeezing.

Chicken Supreme with Mushroom Cream Sauce

This sauce has so much depth of flavour; it's rich with the taste of mushrooms. The key is making a quick stock by rehydrating dried morels in hot water. Dried mushrooms have an intense and concentrated flavour that brings so much to this sauce. It's delicious with chicken, but equally good with steak and pork chops too. Chicken supreme is a classic French cut: a breast that has part of the wing bone attached and the skin still on. It's got great flavour, retains moisture when it's cooked and looks great on the plate as well.

SERVES: 4
PREP TIME: 10–15 MINUTES, PLUS 30 MINUTES SOAKING
COOKING TIME: ABOUT 1 HOUR

FOR THE MUSHROOM CREAM SAUCE
10g dried morels
(or mixed dried mushrooms)
2 tbsp olive oil
60g butter
2 small banana shallots, thinly sliced
2 garlic cloves, crushed
2 sprigs of fresh thyme
3 sprigs of fresh tarragon
75ml Madeira
200ml good-quality chicken stock
100ml double cream
400g mixed mushrooms (such as oyster, chestnut, shiitake), sliced
2 tbsp finely chopped fresh tarragon

1. Preheat the oven to 200°C/180°C fan/gas 6.

2. Start by soaking the dried mushrooms for the sauce. Place the morel mushrooms into a jug and cover with 200ml of hot water from the kettle. Allow to steep and rehydrate for around 30 minutes.

3. Meanwhile, heat 1 tablespoon of the olive oil and half the butter in a large, wide non-stick sauté pan over medium heat. Once hot, add the shallots, garlic and a pinch of salt and pepper and cook for 8–10 minutes until softened. Add the thyme and tarragon sprigs to the pan then pour in the Madeira. Bring to the boil, then reduce the heat to a simmer and cook for 4–5 minutes until reduced and a syrupy consistency.

4. Strain the dried mushrooms and add the mushroom liquor to the pan (discard the dried mushrooms, you just want the intense stock for flavour) and cook for a few minutes before adding the chicken stock. Simmer gently for 15–20 minutes, adding a splash of extra stock if needed to loosen.

Continued Overleaf …

FOR THE CHICKEN

2 tbsp olive oil

4 chicken supreme, skin on

1 garlic bulb, cut in half
horizontally

4 sprigs of fresh thyme

2 bay leaves

sea salt and freshly
ground black pepper

5. Meanwhile, to cook the chicken, heat the olive oil in a pan until hot. Season the chicken supremes with salt and pepper and pan-fry, skin side down for 4–5 minutes, until golden brown. Add the garlic bulb, thyme sprigs and bay leaves to the pan then turn the chicken over and cook for a further 2 minutes. Transfer the chicken, garlic and herbs to a baking tray and cook in the oven for 20–25 minutes until the chicken is cooked through.

6. Remove the thyme and tarragon stalks from the mushroom sauce, then transfer to a blender or food processor. Blitz until smooth, then pass through a sieve into a clean saucepan and stir in the cream.

7. Heat the remaining oil and butter in a large non-stick frying or sauté pan; once melted, add the mushrooms with a good pinch of seasoning and fry over high heat for 4–5 minutes, stirring frequently until golden and softened. Stir through the tarragon and heat through. Add these sautéed mushrooms to the cream sauce and warm gently.

8. To serve, arrange the chicken supremes on serving plates. Spoon the mushroom sauce alongside and serve with greens of your choice.

MARCUS'S TIP

If you can't get hold of chicken supremes, I recommend using skin-on, bone-in thighs instead. Or switch up your usual gravy on your Sunday roast, as this sauce is also delicious with roast potatoes and veg!

White Fish with Hazelnut Crumb and Hollandaise Sauce

Hollandaise sauce is so wonderfully versatile. It's delicious poured on top of poached eggs for breakfast or brunch and it pairs perfectly with steak and all types of fish for a fabulous lunch or dinner. If it splits, simply add a few drops of cold water to the mixture and keep whisking until it all comes back together. Such a simple trick that works every time.

SERVES: 4 AS A STARTER
PREP TIME: 30 MINUTES
COOKING TIME: ABOUT 30 MINUTES

30g butter, cubed

75g blanched hazelnuts

2 slices of sourdough (about 75g), torn into small pieces

4 cod or haddock fillets, skin removed

olive oil

sea salt and freshly ground black pepper

wedges of lemon and fresh parsley sprigs, to serve

FOR THE HOLLANDAISE
2 shallots, sliced

100ml white wine

1 bay leaf

3 sprigs of fresh thyme

40ml white wine vinegar

¼ tsp fennel seeds

250g butter, cubed

3 egg yolks

1. To make the hollandaise reduction, put the shallots, wine, herbs, vinegar and fennel seeds into a saucepan and bring to the boil. Cook for 6–8 minutes until reduced to a third, then strain into a jug and discard the shallots and herbs.

2. Preheat the oven to 200°C/180°C fan/gas 6.

3. Put the 30g butter into a small roasting dish with the hazelnuts and sourdough. Season lightly and bake for 10–15 minutes, stirring halfway, until golden. Remove (leaving the oven on), allow to cool, then roughly chop.

4. For the hollandaise, begin by melting the 250g butter in a medium saucepan over medium-high heat. When it has melted and is foaming remove from the heat and set aside. Cool until warm to the touch.

5. Place the egg yolks in a large stainless steel or heatproof glass bowl. Bring a third of a saucepan of water to a very gentle simmer. Place the bowl of egg yolks over the pan, making sure it doesn't touch the water, and whisk by hand until they are thick and ribbons form. Very slowly add a little of the melted butter, whisking continuously. Keep adding small amounts of the butter, whisking well between additions, then when the hollandaise begins to thicken, add 1 tablespoon of the reduction, whisk again, add another tablespoon, whisk until smooth, then continue adding the butter. Taste the sauce and add more reduction if needed. Season with sea salt.

6. Place the fish fillets onto a baking tray, drizzle with a little olive oil, season, then scatter the crumbs over the top of the fillets. Bake for 8–10 minutes, or until the fish is just cooked.

7. Serve the crumbed fish with the hollandaise, lemon wedges and parsley sprigs.

Compound Butters

'Compound butters' is a cheffy way of saying flavoured butters. These are an amazing culinary trick to have up your sleeve, allowing you to add a real flavour punch to all sorts of things with almost no effort at all. Make a few different flavours and keep them in the freezer, that way you can just slice off what you need, when you need it. Herby garlic butter is delicious with fish, garlic bread and pasta, spiced butter is incredible melted on top of a resting steak and sweetened butter will elevate your sponge cake buttercream frosting to the next level.

MAKES: 250G
PREP TIME: 5 MINUTES, PLUS 2 HOURS CHILLING

FOR HERBED GARLIC BUTTER

250g soft butter

1 tsp good-quality flaked sea salt

a good grinding of black pepper

grated zest of 1 lemon

4 sprigs of fresh thyme, leaves picked and finely chopped

2 sprigs of fresh flat-leaf parsley, leaves picked and finely chopped

1 sprig of fresh oregano, leaves picked and finely chopped

1 or 2 garlic cloves, crushed

FOR SWEETENED BUTTER

250g soft butter

pinch of sea salt

2 tsp ground cinnamon

4 tbsp soft light brown sugar

grated zest of 1 orange

FOR SPICED BUTTER

250g soft butter

1 tsp good-quality flaked sea salt

a good grinding of black pepper

2 sprigs of fresh rosemary, leaves picked and finely chopped

3 sprigs of fresh thyme, leaves picked and finely chopped

2 sprigs of fresh flat-leaf parsley, leaves picked and finely chopped

1 red chilli, deseeded and finely chopped

1 tsp smoked paprika

2 garlic cloves, crushed

1. Combine the soft butter in a bowl with the other ingredients and mix together with the back of a fork until well combined.

2. Tip the flavoured butter onto a sheet of baking parchment and roll up tightly into a log, then twist the ends up tightly. Chill in the fridge for at least 2 hours before using.

3. If not using immediately the wrapped log will keep in the fridge for up to 1 week or the freezer for up to 3 months.

Chicken Liver Parfait

A parfait is essentially an extra smooth pâté. In this case, the ingredients are blended, passed through a sieve and then whipped to achieve a light and creamy texture. Once you're comfortable with the technique, you can experiment with the flavours, adding different herbs or spices such as nutmeg or sage. Make this in a large dish or in individual ramekins for a dinner party starter – either way serve with plenty of bread to smear it on.

SERVES: 6–8 AS A STARTER
PREP TIME: 20 MINUTES,
PLUS 2 HOURS CHILLING
COOKING TIME: ABOUT 20 MINUTES

400g chicken livers

200g butter, melted

4 shallots, thinly sliced

bunch of fresh thyme

2 garlic cloves, crushed

100ml white wine

2 tbsp brandy

50ml double cream

100ml clarified butter, melted (see page 37)

few sprigs of fresh thyme, to finish

sea salt and freshly ground black pepper

TO SERVE
baguette, thinly sliced and toasted

1. Get your food processor ready and place an oval pie dish (approx. 18cm in length and 3–4cm deep) in the fridge to chill. Prepare a large bowl of iced water.

2. Wash the chicken livers under cold running water and pat them dry with kitchen paper. Trim off any sinew and cut larger livers in half.

3. Add 2 tablespoons of the butter to a large frying pan over medium heat. When hot, add the shallots and bunch of thyme, season well with sea salt, and cook for 5–7 minutes until soft and golden. Add the garlic and fry for another minute. Add the wine and brandy and cook for 3–4 minutes until reduced by half. Remove and discard the thyme and transfer the mix to the food processor.

4. Add 2 more tablespoons of butter to the frying pan. Place over high heat and when hot, season the livers and fry them in two batches for about 1 minute each side, until golden but not cooked through (they should be lightly pink on the inside but not bloody). Add them to the food processor and blend.

5. Pour the remaining melted butter and cream into the food processor and blend until smooth. Taste and season if necessary.

6. Pass the paste through a fine sieve into a bowl on top of the bowl of iced water. Whisk the pâté until it starts to cool, then transfer to the pie dish. Cover with clingfilm and chill.

7. Pour the clarified butter over the top in an even layer and arrange a few thyme sprigs on top. Chill the pâté for at least 2 hours, or until it is completely cold and has set. Serve with toasted baguette.

Pork and Pheasant Terrine

Terrines aren't quite as fashionable now as they were when I was at college. They have a reputation for being complex and time consuming to make, but I absolutely love them and have the perfect stress-free recipe using clarified butter, which adds incredible richness and decadence. Once you've mastered the technique of terrine making the world is your oyster. You can switch up the spices and flavours you use as well as the meats, for example adding duck or chicken in place of pheasant if that's hard to find.

SERVES: 8–10 AS A STARTER
PREP TIME: 30 MINUTES,
PLUS OVERNIGHT CHILLING
COOKING TIME: ABOUT 2 HOURS

250ml port

1 pheasant breast, skinned

500g pork shoulder, diced into small 1cm pieces

200g duck livers, roughly chopped

finely grated zest of 1 orange

2 tsp ground allspice

½ nutmeg, grated

½ tsp ground cinnamon

200g butter, to cover

2–3 sprigs of fresh thyme, leaves picked

sea salt and freshly ground black pepper

TO SERVE

drizzle of extra virgin olive oil

chopped pistachio nuts

sliced baguette

1. Put the port in a small saucepan and bring to the boil. Simmer until reduced by half, then remove from the heat and leave to cool.

2. Finely chop the pheasant breast and put into the bowl of a food processor. Add the diced pork shoulder and pulse to break down the meat until coarsely minced. Add the duck livers and blitz again.

3. Transfer to a large bowl and mix in the reduced port, orange zest, spices, a pinch of sea salt and some freshly ground black pepper. Mix well.

4. Lightly grease a 1 litre lidded terrine mould or loaf tin with a little of the butter, then line it with a sheet of baking parchment twice the size of the tin.

5. Preheat the oven to 150°C/130°C fan/gas 2. Spoon the mixture into the lined terrine, pressing down into the edges of the dish.

6. Cover with a lid (or baking parchment and foil) and place the terrine into a small roasting tin. Add enough just-boiled water to the roasting tin to come 2cm up the outside of the terrine. Bake in the centre of the oven for 1½ hours.

7. To test if the terrine is ready, remove from the oven and insert a skewer into the centre. Hold for 10 seconds, then remove and lightly touch the end – the skewer should feel hot. The terrine should have also shrunk away from the sides of the dish.

8. Remove from the roasting tin, then take off the terrine lid and drain off the liquid released during cooking. Cover with a double layer of foil and leave to cool, then put a heavy weight on top (such as a couple of tins of beans). Chill in the fridge overnight.

9. Melt the butter in a small saucepan over medium-high heat until the solids start to float to the surface; skim off and discard, then pour the clarified butter over the set terrine. Press a few thyme leaves into the butter and chill for another hour or until set.

10. Once it has set turn the terrine out onto a board, with the butter layer at the top and cut into thick slices. Drizzle with extra virgin olive oil, season with salt and pepper and scatter over the pistachio nuts. Serve with sliced baguette.

Confit de Canard

Confit is a French technique for preserving food; essentially it means to cook
and store ingredients in fat. But as well as preserving, it's an amazing way to cook
tougher cuts of meat that benefit from long, slow cooking. Perhaps the most
famous ingredient to confit is duck, which is one of the first recipes I learned back
in my college days, but it's a technique that can be applied to lots of different
things like tomatoes, onions, pork belly and even egg yolks.

SERVES: 4
PREP TIME: 20 MINUTES,
PLUS 4 HOURS SALTING
COOKING TIME: ABOUT 4–5 HOURS

4 duck legs, skin on

100g rock salt

700–750g duck fat

¼ bunch of fresh thyme

2 bay leaves

FOR THE MUSTARD DRESSING

1 tsp Dijon mustard

2 tbsp white wine vinegar

6 tbsp extra virgin olive oil

pinch of caster sugar

sea salt and freshly
ground black pepper

TO SERVE

green salad

baguette, torn or sliced

1. Lay the duck legs, skin side up, in a shallow bowl or tray. Sprinkle over the rock salt and leave in the fridge for about 4 hours.

2. Rinse the salt from the duck legs and pat dry. Preheat the oven to 150°C/130°C fan/gas 2.

3. Heat 700g duck fat in a 23 × 23cm roasting tray over medium heat until melted. Add the thyme, bay leaves and duck legs, skin side down, ensuring the duck is covered in the fat. If not, add some more duck fat. Cover with foil and slow cook in the oven for 4–5 hours until the duck is tender. Allow to cool slightly, then carefully remove the legs from the fat.

4. Increase the oven temperature to 220°C/200°C fan/gas 7.

5. Put the duck in a clean roasting tin and roast, skin side up, on the top shelf, for 10 minutes. If the skin isn't crisp enough, finish it off under a hot grill.

6. Meanwhile, make the mustard dressing. Place the Dijon mustard, white wine vinegar, extra virgin olive oil, caster sugar and some salt and pepper into a jar and then shake until it is emulsified. Taste and add a little more sugar or mustard if you think it needs it.

7. Serve the duck legs with a green salad dressed with the mustard dressing and baguette on the side.

Tournedos Rossini

If you think French food has a reputation for being rich, decadent and indulgent, this dish could be the reason why! You don't see it much on menus these days, but it was created in the early 1800s by a chef called Marie-Antoine Carême; the original includes foie gras and truffles as well as the fillet steak and Madeira sauce. I've lightened it up a little but retained the essence of this really special and uniquely French recipe.

SERVES: 4
PREP TIME: 20 MINUTES
COOKING TIME: ABOUT 45 MINUTES

4 x 2cm-thick slices of
white bread or brioche

30g butter

4 x 200g fillet steaks

1 tbsp olive oil

50g Chicken Liver Parfait
(page 34), or shopbought

300g baby spinach

sea salt and freshly
ground black pepper

FOR THE MADEIRA SAUCE
50g butter

2 banana shallots, thinly sliced

2 tsp cornflour or plain flour

125ml Madeira

500ml homemade or good-quality
beef stock (not from a stock cube)

handful of fresh thyme

1. First make the Madeira sauce. Melt a tablespoon of the butter in a saucepan, add the sliced shallots, season well and cook over medium heat until softened but not coloured. Add the cornflour or plain flour and cook for another minute. Add the Madeira and cook over high heat for 5 minutes, or until the liquid has reduced by half.

2. Add the beef stock and thyme and simmer over medium heat for 15 minutes, or until the sauce has reduced by half and thickened. Whisk in the remaining butter a little at a time and season to taste.

3. Next prepare the toast. Cut the bread into 10–12cm circles (or just larger than the width of the fillet steak) using a round pastry cutter. Heat 1 tablespoon of the butter in a frying pan over medium heat and fry the bread slices on both sides until golden. Set aside.

4. Heat a little olive oil in the same frying pan over medium heat. Season one side of the steaks and place them seasoned side down in the pan. Cook for about 3 minutes, season the second side and turn them over. Cook for a further 3 minutes until medium-rare. Add the remaining butter to the pan and use the melted butter to baste the steaks. Remove from the pan, loosely cover with foil and allow to rest in a warm place for 10 minutes.

5. Place the spinach leaves into the same pan over medium heat and stir until wilted. Season and drain away any excess water.

6. Spread each toast with a little chicken liver parfait, top with some wilted spinach, a cooked steak and pour over a little of the Madeira sauce. Serve immediately.

Quiche Lorraine

I remember learning how to make shortcrust pastry in college and being amazed by how many recipes it unlocked – there really are endless possibilities for it. I know these days you can buy decent ready-made shortcrust, but unlike puff pastry, it really is very quick and easy to make your own so I would encourage you to master the art. One of my favourite French things to make with it is a quiche Lorraine with lots of bacon and onions. You will need a fluted, loose-bottomed tart tin, 23cm in diameter and 3cm deep. Photographed overleaf.

SERVES: 6–8
PREP TIME: 25 MINUTES,
PLUS 35 MINUTES CHILLING
COOKING TIME: 45–50 MINUTES

FOR THE PASTRY
250g plain flour,
plus extra for dusting

½ tsp fine salt

125g cold butter, cut into cubes

1 egg yolk

2–3 tbsp cold water

FOR THE FILLING
1 tbsp olive oil

1 large onion, thinly sliced

1 tbsp fresh thyme leaves

150g smoked bacon lardons

100g Gruyère cheese, grated

300ml double cream

3 eggs

sea salt and freshly ground black pepper

TO SERVE
green salad

1. First make the pastry. Put the flour, salt and butter into a food processor and blitz until the mixture resembles breadcrumbs. Add the egg yolk then the water, a little at a time, and blend until it comes together in a smooth ball. Turn out onto a lightly floured work surface, roll into a disc, wrap in clingfilm and chill for 20 minutes.

2. Preheat the oven to 200°C/180°C fan/gas 6.

3. Place the rested pastry dough onto a lightly floured work surface and roll to the thickness of 5mm and wide enough to cover the tart tin with 1–2cm hanging over the edge. Sprinkle your rolling pin with a little more flour and then carefully lift the pastry onto the pin and then into the tart tin. Dip your fingers in a little flour so they don't stick to the pastry then carefully press the pastry into the base and into the grooved sides of the tin – the pastry will hang over the edges a little. Be careful not to stretch the pastry as this will cause tears or make the pastry shrink in the oven.

4. Prick the pastry base a few times with a fork so it doesn't puff up during baking. Cut a circle of baking parchment a little larger than the tin, place on top of the pastry so it overhangs a little and fill this with ceramic baking beans or uncooked rice/dried beans. Place in the fridge and chill for at least 10–15 minutes, or until the pastry is firm to touch.

5. Place the tin onto a baking sheet and 'blind bake' for 15 minutes. Remove the baking parchment and baking beans and bake for another 5 minutes, or until the pastry is evenly golden and crisp. Remove from the oven and allow to cool slightly. When cool enough to handle, trim away the excess pastry from the edges of the tart case with a small sharp knife. Reduce the oven temperature to 190°C/170°C fan/gas 5.

6. To make the filling, heat the oil in a frying pan and gently fry the onion and thyme leaves over low heat. Season with salt and pepper and cook until softened but not coloured. Remove from the heat and set aside to cool. Fry the bacon lardons in the same frying pan until golden and crisp.

7. Scatter the softened onions over the blind baked tart base and add half the cooked bacon and half the grated Gruyère.

8. Pour the cream into a jug, add the eggs, season and whisk together. Pour the egg and cream mix over the onions, then scatter with the remaining cooked bacon and grated Gruyère.

9. Carefully place the quiche on a baking sheet and bake for 25–30 minutes, or until just set. It will continue cooking in the residual heat so remove from the oven while it still has a little wobble. Allow to cool in the tin for 10 minutes, then remove and serve warm with a green salad.

MARCUS'S TIP

For a vegetarian version try adding sautéed leeks instead of the bacon and if you want to ramp up the flavour even more, you could add chopped rosemary or thyme leaves to the pastry.

Mushroom Duxelles

We are all probably most familiar with duxelles as one of the layers in a classic beef Wellington, but this French technique for cooking mushrooms can be used in many different ways, not least as an extra layer of deliciousness in a Quiche Lorraine! Also, served with small toasts it makes a fantastic vegetarian alternative to terrines and pâtés and it can be used as a filling for omelettes, a stuffing for chicken breasts – even stirred through pasta or a risotto. The type of mushroom doesn't matter so use whatever is available to you.

SERVES: 6
PREP TIME: 10 MINUTES
COOKING TIME: ABOUT 20 MINUTES

450g button or
chestnut mushrooms

25g butter

2 banana shallots, finely chopped

few sprigs of fresh thyme,
leaves picked and chopped

2 garlic cloves, finely chopped

small bunch each of fresh parsley
and tarragon, leaves picked
and finely chopped

1–2 tbsp cognac

sea salt and freshly
ground black pepper

1. Wipe the mushrooms clean with kitchen paper. Cut the mushrooms into quarters, add to a food processor and pulse a few times until finely chopped.

2. Melt the butter in a sauté pan over medium-low heat, add the shallots and thyme leaves, season well and fry for 3–4 minutes, or until softened. Add the garlic and cook for another minute.

3. Add the mushrooms and cook until most of the moisture that has been released has evaporated – this will take 10–15 minutes. Stir in the parsley and tarragon and then the cognac and cook until the alcohol has evaporated. Taste and adjust the seasoning.

4. Spoon into a bowl and leave to cool.

Churros with Lavender Sugar and Citrus Cream

Called *pâte à choux* in French, this type of pastry has a fabulously light texture, which comes from the addition of lots of eggs. It's the basis for profiteroles, croquembouche, eclairs and Paris-Brest – all incredible, classic French desserts. I wanted to do something a bit different so instead of baking it, I've deep-fried it, turning it into a French version of churros. I'm so pleased with how this turned out, I urge you to try it. Photographed overleaf.

MAKES: ABOUT 30–35
PREP TIME: 40 MINUTES
COOKING TIME: 30 MINUTES

FOR THE CHURROS
150g cold butter, cubed

25g caster sugar

½ tsp fine sea salt

250g plain flour

4–5 eggs

2 tsp edible lavender heads, plus extra to decorate

150g golden caster sugar

vegetable oil, for deep frying

FOR THE CITRUS SYRUP
150g caster sugar

juice of 1 lemon

juice of 1 orange

1 tbsp cognac (optional)

300ml whipping cream

1. Put 250ml of water, the butter, sugar and salt in a saucepan, place over low heat and bring to the boil. Remove from the heat just as it starts to boil (don't allow the water to boil for long as it will evaporate, which will affect the consistency of the choux pastry and make it too thick).

2. Tip the flour into the pan and use a wooden spoon to beat until it forms a paste which comes away from the sides of the saucepan. Set aside until it is cool to the touch.

3. Add the eggs one at a time, beating after each addition with a wooden spoon until it is well combined. The paste should be smooth and shiny and if you lift up the spoon it should slowly drop off – it needs to be thick but also pipeable. If it is very stiff add a little more egg.

4. Blend the lavender heads with the sugar in a small blender until they are well combined and then tip onto a large plate and set aside.

5. Make the citrus syrup. Put the caster sugar into a saucepan. Remove the skin from the lemon and orange using a vegetable peeler and then cut the skin into very thin julienne strips with a sharp knife.

6. Place these julienne strips into the saucepan and add the lemon and orange juices. Place over medium heat and simmer for 5 minutes, or until the liquid has reduced by half and it has turned a little syrupy. Stir in the cognac (if using). Remove from the heat and then pass through a sieve, reserving a few of the citrus julienne strips to decorate.

Continued Overleaf…

7. Whip the cream until it forms soft peaks, then once the syrup has cooled completely, swirl it through the cream. Top with the reserved julienne pieces if you like.

8. Half-fill a medium saucepan with vegetable oil and place over medium heat. Heat to 180°C, or until a cube of bread sizzles and turns golden in 30 seconds.

9. Put the choux paste into a piping bag fitted with a star nozzle. Working in small batches, carefully pipe strips of the mixture into the hot oil, using scissors to snip off 10cm lengths. Fry for 3–4 minutes, carefully flip over using a slotted spoon and fry for another minute or two, or until the churros are golden brown. Remove with a slotted spoon, drain on kitchen paper for a few seconds and then place – while still hot – onto the plate of lavender sugar. Roll around in the sugar and then set aside. Repeat until all of the choux paste is used up.

10. Serve the hot churros, scattered with a few extra lavender heads, with the citrus whipped cream on the side for dipping.

St Clements Citrus Tart

The ingredients and method for sweet pastry are almost identical to regular shortcrust; unsurprisingly the only difference is the addition of sugar. This pastry recipe can be used for all manner of desserts from lemon meringue pie and treacle tart to pecan pie, but this is my take on the classic French tarte au citron, with the addition of orange to make it extra delicious. You will need a 23cm fluted, loose-bottomed tart tin.

SERVES: 8–10
PREP TIME: 20 MINUTES, PLUS 50 MINUTES CHILLING
COOKING TIME: ABOUT 1 HOUR 10 MINUTES

FOR THE PASTRY
175g plain flour, plus extra for dusting
pinch of fine sea salt
115g cold butter, cubed
50g icing sugar
1 egg yolk
1–2 tbsp cold water

FOR THE FILLING
5 eggs
175g caster sugar
150ml double cream
grated zest and juice of 2 lemons
finely grated zest of 1 orange

1. To make the pastry, rub together the flour, salt and cold butter in a bowl until the mixture has a breadcrumb-like texture (or blitz in a food processor). Stir in the icing sugar and gradually add the egg yolk and cold water to form a soft, pliable dough. Shape the dough into a disc, wrap in clingfilm and chill for 30 minutes.

2. Preheat the oven to 210°C/190°C fan/gas 7.

3. Place the rested pastry dough onto a lightly floured work surface and roll out until it is 3–5mm thick and wide enough to cover a 23cm fluted, loose-bottomed tart tin with 1–2cm hanging over the edge. Sprinkle your rolling pin with a little more flour and then carefully lift the pastry onto the pin and then into the tart tin. Dip your fingers in a little flour so they don't stick to the pastry, then carefully press the pastry into the base and grooves in the sides of the tin, leaving a little excess pastry to hang over the edges. Be careful not to stretch the pastry as this will cause tears or make the pastry shrink in the oven.

4. Prick the pastry base a few times with a fork so it doesn't puff up during baking. Cut a circle of baking parchment a little larger than the tin, place on top of the pastry so it overhangs a little and fill this with ceramic baking beans or uncooked rice/dried beans. Place in the fridge and chill for 20 minutes, or until the pastry is firm to touch.

TO SERVE

sifted icing sugar

4–5 passionfruit, halved

5. Place the tin onto a baking sheet and 'blind bake' for 15 minutes. Remove the baking parchment and baking beans and bake for another 5 minutes, or until the pastry is golden and crisp. Remove from the oven and allow to cool slightly. When cool enough to handle, trim away the excess pastry from the edges of the tart case with a small sharp knife and set aside to cool fully. Reduce the oven temperature to 140°C/120°C fan/gas 1.

6. For the filling, whisk the eggs and sugar in a bowl until they are completely combined. Add the cream, lemon zest and juice and orange zest and lightly whisk to combine.

7. Carefully pour the mixture into the cooled and trimmed tart case and bake for 45–50 minutes, or until set.

8. Remove the tart from the oven. Carefully remove from the tin and leave to cool completely. Just before serving, dust with some sifted icing sugar and cut into slices. Serve each slice with half a passionfruit scooped over the top.

MARCUS'S TIP

Once you've mastered making this sweet pastry recipe you can have a go at experimenting with different flavours to impress your friends and family. I sometimes use lavender- or vanilla-infused sugar in place of the regular caster to make it extra special. And for an even more intense hit of citrus, try adding some orange or lemon zest.

The

Classics

When I was 17, I took part in a competition judged by Jack Neighbour, a senior lecturer at South Trafford College in Manchester. It was another key turning point in my life. After winning my regional heat, Jack connected me with Anton Edelmann, executive chef at The Savoy in central London, who offered me a job. I remember my dad putting me on a train to the capital and telling me not to come back. He knew that becoming a successful, fine dining chef was my dream and he gave me the final push I needed to fly the nest. And what a world I had flown into! I thought I knew what hard work was from all the years I spent working with my old man in his warehouse, but this was another level. There were times in this phase of my career when I'd work six days a week from 7am until midnight. I'd met Jane by then; she was living in Kent and would often drive into London to pick me up at 1am on a Sunday. Then I'd be on the 5am train back to London on Monday morning.

It was during these years that I truly honed my skills and learned how to cook so many incredible classic French dishes. Classics are classics for a reason: they've stood the test of time and they're cooked in restaurants and homes over and over again. They're recipes that work, comfort, satisfy and excite.

In this chapter I want to share some of my absolute favourites and arm you with a culinary repertoire to impress anyone from hungry children to dinner party guests. I've taken out some of the lengthy processes and unnecessarily complicated methods to give you user-friendly recipes that don't compromise on taste.

Omelette Arnold Bennett

Beef Tartare

Lobster Thermidor

Clams Marinière

Potato Croquettes with French 'Chimichurri' Sauce

Quick Coq au Vin

Chicken Chasseur

French Onion Stew with Cheesy Thyme Croutons

Beef Fillet Bourguignon

Torte de Gibier with Madeira and Truffle Sauce

Potatoes 3 Ways: Dauphinoise Potatoes,
Pommes Lyonnaise, Pommes Mousseline

Lavender Peach Melba

Apple Tarte Tatin with Nutmeg Cream

Gooseberry, Elderflower and Rosemary
Bavarois with Almond Praline

Omelette Arnold Bennett

This is a dish that I learned at The Savoy, which is perhaps unsurprising as that's where it was invented back in the 1920s. It was created for the author Arnold Bennett who was staying at the hotel while writing a novel and it's said to have become his favourite breakfast. The omelette itself provides a base for flaked, smoked haddock, cheese and a rich sauce of hollandaise mixed with whipped cream, which is then grilled until golden and bubbly. It's a great centrepiece for a celebratory breakfast or brunch spread.

SERVES: 4
PREP TIME: 15–20 MINUTES
COOKING TIME: ABOUT 30 MINUTES

FOR THE HADDOCK
300ml milk
2 bay leaves
2 sprigs of fresh thyme
½ tsp peppercorns
3 whole cloves
400g undyed smoked haddock, skin on

FOR THE HOLLANDAISE
3 egg yolks
175g butter, melted
1 tsp white wine vinegar
75ml double cream, lightly whipped

FOR THE OMELETTE
8 eggs
knob of butter
80g Gruyère cheese, finely grated
sea salt and freshly ground black pepper

TO SERVE
green salad
crusty bread

1. Firstly, cook the haddock. Place the milk, bay leaves, thyme, peppercorns and cloves into a wide shallow pan and gently bring to the boil. Add the haddock, reduce the heat to a gentle simmer and poach for 5–6 minutes until the haddock is cooked. Remove from the heat, transfer the haddock to a plate and when cool enough to handle, remove the skin and flake into large pieces. Set the fish aside (discard the poaching liquor).

2. To make the hollandaise sauce, add the egg yolks to a large heatproof glass bowl set over a saucepan of simmering water. Whisk the yolks until pale and fluffy, taking care not to overcook them, and gradually whisk in half the melted butter, whisking constantly. Remove the bowl from the heat, add the white wine vinegar, then return the bowl to the heat and whisk in the remaining melted butter. Remove from the heat and allow to sit for a minute or two before gently folding in the whipped cream. Set aside.

3. Preheat the grill to high.

4. To make the omelette, beat the eggs in a large bowl and season with salt and pepper. Heat a 26cm non-stick frying pan over medium heat and add a knob of butter. Once melted, pour in the egg mixture and cook, stirring continually and slowly until the eggs are just beginning to set, but still a little runny in the middle. Remove from the heat and scatter over the flaked haddock followed by the cheese. Pour over the hollandaise sauce.

5. Place the pan under the grill and cook for 2–3 minutes until the top is golden brown and bubbling.

6. Serve the omelette with a green salad and chunks of crusty bread.

Beef Tartare

This dish is a real retro favourite, made with finely diced raw beef. You'll often find it being prepared table-side as a starter at fancy French restaurants and it's classically served with a raw egg yolk on top – not for the faint-hearted! I've kept the flavours of my tartare traditional, but have updated it with more of a brunch vibe, serving it with a perfectly poached egg.

SERVES: 2
PREP TIME: 30 MINUTES
COOKING TIME: ABOUT 5 MINUTES

200g beef steak
(fillet, sirloin or bavette)

10g capers, drained and chopped

1 small shallot, finely chopped (15g)

20g cornichons, finely chopped
(approx. 2 small ones)

2 tbsp chopped fresh flat-leaf parsley

1 tbsp olive oil

a few drops each of Tabasco
and Worcestershire sauce

2 eggs

a few drops of white wine vinegar

sea salt and freshly ground
black pepper

toasted baguette, to serve

1. To prepare the tartare, finely chop the steak of your choice into small dice (or whatever size you prefer), discarding any fat. Add the capers, shallot, cornichons and parsley and season with ½ teaspoon sea salt and some pepper. Add the olive oil, Tabasco and Worcestershire sauces and mix together. Return the mixture to the fridge in a bowl to keep it as cold as possible.

2. To poach the eggs, bring a large saucepan of water to the boil and add a good pinch of salt. Crack the eggs into two ramekins, adding a few drops of vinegar to each. Whisk the boiling water so it swirls in a whirlpool, turn the heat down to a gentle simmer then slide in the eggs. Poach for 3–4 minutes, remove with a slotted spoon and set aside on a warm plate.

3. Divide the tartare between two serving plates, pressing it into the bottom of a large ring cutter. Remove the cutter and top each tartare with a poached egg, seasoning the egg with salt and pepper. Serve the tartare with toasted baguette alongside.

MARCUS'S TIP

If you want to get ahead with this dish, you can poach your eggs in advance. Poach the eggs as in step 2 but once cooked, plunge them into a bowl of iced water. When you're ready to serve, simply put them back into a pan of hot water to warm them through for 30 seconds.

Lobster Thermidor

This is a deceptively easy dish to put together and the results are simply spectacular: talk about a showstopper. The roux-based sauce has loads of added flavour and is then mixed with cooked lobster meat and topped with cheese. Its history is a little unclear – some say it originated in a Parisian restaurant in the 1800s and others say it was named by Napoleon Bonaparte. All I know is that when I learned how to make it in the 1980s, it was the height of sophistication. I still love it to this day.

SERVES: 4
PREP TIME: 30 MINUTES
COOKING TIME: ABOUT 20 MINUTES

500ml milk

3 bay leaves

1 small onion, thickly sliced

6 black peppercorns

2 cooked lobsters (approx. 750g each)

90g butter

2 tbsp plain flour

2 shallots, finely chopped

240ml dry white wine

1 heaped tsp Dijon mustard

1 tbsp chopped fresh tarragon

1 tbsp chopped fresh chives

2 tbsp double cream

pinch of cayenne pepper

100g Gruyère cheese, finely grated

sea salt and freshly ground black pepper

green salad, to serve

1. Preheat the grill to high.

2. Put the milk, bay leaves, onion and peppercorns in a small saucepan, place over low heat and bring to the boil. Remove from the heat and leave to infuse for 10 minutes, then strain through a sieve and discard the bay leaves, peppercorns and onion.

3. Meanwhile, remove the lobster meat from the cooked lobster and cut it into bite-size pieces. Clean out the lobster shells and place them on a shallow baking tray.

4. Melt 30g of the butter in another small saucepan, stir in the flour and cook for a minute. Pour in a little of the infused milk and whisk until smooth. Gradually whisk in the rest of the milk and bring to the boil, then reduce the heat and simmer for 5 minutes, stirring occasionally, or until thickened to the consistency of thick cream.

5. While the sauce is simmering melt the remaining butter in another small saucepan, add the shallots and cook over gentle heat until soft but not browned. Add the wine, increase the heat and simmer rapidly until you are left with a tablespoonful or two of liquid. Stir in the white sauce, together with the mustard, tarragon, chives, cream, cayenne pepper and half the grated cheese. Season to taste with salt and black pepper.

6. Stir the lobster meat into the sauce, then divide the mixture equally among the cleaned half-shells. Sprinkle with the remaining cheese, slide under the grill and cook for 3–4 minutes until golden and bubbling. Serve with a crisp green salad.

Clams Marinière

A classic marinière uses mussels rather than clams, but I wanted to shake things up a bit and found that if you apply exactly the same method and ingredients for the sauce, it's just as delicious and makes a nice change from the original. I love making a huge pot of clams marinière and plonking it in the middle of the dinner table for people to help themselves, along with plenty of crusty French bread to soak up all those amazing juices. I like to add samphire to mine, but it would be just as good without it.

SERVES: 4
PREP TIME: 25 MINUTES
COOKING TIME: ABOUT 30 MINUTES

2kg clams such as palourde

100g butter, diced

4 shallots, thinly sliced

2 bay leaves

150ml white wine

150ml dry cider

½ tsp table salt

150ml good-quality chicken or vegetable stock

100g samphire

¼ bunch of fresh tarragon, leaves chopped

sea salt and freshly ground black pepper

crusty bread, to serve

1. Rinse the clams well in a colander under cold running water to remove any grit. Use a vegetable brush to scrub off any visible barnacles and dirt. If any of the clams are open, tap them hard against a work surface and if they don't close, discard them.

2. Melt 50g of the butter in a large saucepan (with a lid), big enough to fit all of the clams, over medium heat. Add the shallots and bay leaves and cook for 5–7 minutes until the shallots are soft but not browned, then add the wine, cider and table salt. Bring to the boil and simmer for 10 minutes, then add the stock. Simmer for a further 5 minutes then add the cleaned clams, cover with the lid and cook over high heat for 4 minutes. Remove the lid and check that most of the clams have opened – if quite a few are still closed, replace the lid and cook for a further minute. Strain the liquor into a medium saucepan and keep the clams hot in the large saucepan, covered with the lid. Discard any unopened clams.

3. Bring the liquor to the boil and gradually whisk in the remaining 50g butter, cube by cube, until you have a thickened and flavoursome sauce.

4. Add the samphire to the sauce and simmer for 2 minutes, then stir in the tarragon. Season to taste with salt and pepper.

5. Divide the clams among four large bowls and spoon over the sauce. Serve with crusty bread.

Potato Croquettes with French 'Chimichurri' Sauce

French croquettes are the most amazing snack. Unlike their Spanish counterparts, they are made with mashed potato. You can add all sorts of flavours to the mixture like ham and sautéed mushrooms – I've even made them with snails before and I'd encourage you to be bold and try them yourself! But for the purposes of this recipe, I've kept the flavour of the croquettes themselves classic and served them with a punchy, herby dip. Photographed overleaf.

MAKES: 26–28
PREP TIME: 40 MINUTES,
PLUS COOLING AND 3 HOURS
30 MINUTES CHILLING
COOKING TIME: ABOUT 1 HOUR

FOR THE CROQUETTES
450g floury potatoes
(such as Maris Piper)
15g butter
1 onion, finely diced
1 tbsp fresh thyme leaves
50g Gruyère cheese, grated
vegetable oil, for deep-frying
sea salt and freshly
ground black pepper

FOR THE CHEESE SAUCE
250ml milk
25g butter
25g plain flour
100g Gruyère cheese, grated
2 tsp Dijon mustard

1. Preheat the oven to 200°C/180°C fan/gas 6.

2. Scrub the potatoes, pierce them with a fork and place them on a baking tray. Bake in the oven for 35–40 minutes until soft. Slice a cross in the top of each one to allow the steam to escape; when cool enough to handle, scoop out the flesh and pass it through a sieve, mouli or potato ricer into a bowl. Set aside.

3. While the potatoes are baking, make the cheese sauce. Put the milk in a small saucepan and gently bring to the boil over low heat. Melt the butter in another pan and add the flour and a pinch of salt and pepper. Cook, stirring, over low heat for about 1 minute, stirring to prevent it from browning. Add a ladle of the hot milk and stir to combine. Continue adding the milk a bit at a time until you have a thick sauce. Bring to a simmer, then stir in the cheese and mustard until melted. Remove from the heat and then transfer to a large bowl.

4. Heat the 15g butter in a frying pan over medium heat. Add the onion and cook for about 10 minutes until soft but not coloured. Stir in the thyme leaves, then add to the sauce in the bowl. Add the 50g grated cheese to the mashed potato and mix well. Chill for 3 hours until firm.

5. Using wet hands, form the croquette mixture into balls, roughly 20g each. Chill for 20 minutes.

FOR THE CRUMB

40g plain flour, seasoned with salt and pepper

2 eggs, beaten

100g dried breadcrumbs (panko or homemade from stale bread)

FOR THE CHIMICHURRI SAUCE

2 heaped tbsp finely chopped fresh tarragon leaves

½ bunch of fresh flat-leaf parsley, leaves picked (15g)

5g fresh chives, roughly chopped

1 green chilli, deseeded and chopped

grated zest and juice of 1 lemon

70ml extra virgin olive oil

6. Put the crumb ingredients in three bowls. Coat the croquettes in the flour, then the egg, then a generous coating of crumbs. Chill (on a tray) for 10 minutes.

7. While the croquettes are in the fridge, make the chimichurri sauce. Put all the ingredients in a mini food processor or blender and pulse until you have a chunky sauce. Add salt to taste.

8. To deep-fry the croquettes, pour enough vegetable oil into a deep saucepan or deep-fat fryer to come up to about 5cm and place over medium heat. If using a deep-fat fryer or if you have a digital cooking thermometer, heat the oil to 170°C. If not, to check the oil is at the right temperature, drop a 2–3cm cube of bread into the hot oil – it should turn golden and crisp in 1 minute.

9. Carefully lower a batch of croquettes into the hot oil and fry for 4 minutes, or until they rise to the surface with a hissing sound. Lift out carefully with a slotted spoon, drain on kitchen paper and repeat with the remaining croquettes. Serve hot with the chimichurri sauce.

MARCUS'S TIP

When it comes to pané *(which is the French way of saying breading), my biggest tip is to use one hand for the flour and breadcrumbs, and another for the egg, this will prevent both your hands getting breaded themselves!*

Quick Coq au Vin

A classic coq au vin, while utterly delicious, is quite a stagey recipe to prepare. There are lots of different elements that are cooked separately before being added at different times to a casserole dish. With this recipe I've taken out as many of the stages as possible, while ensuring that the end result is just as tasty as the original. It's good enough for a dinner party, but easy enough for a weeknight family dinner.

SERVES: 4–6
PREP TIME: 20 MINUTES
COOKING TIME: ABOUT 2 HOURS 20 MINUTES

4 tbsp duck fat or butter

2 celery sticks, quartered

1 onion, chopped

2 carrots, chopped

4 garlic cloves, finely grated

4 tbsp plain flour

½ tsp table salt

½ tsp freshly ground black pepper

1 whole large chicken, jointed into 8 pieces

250g smoked streaky bacon, cut into 1cm lardons

250g button mushrooms, halved if large

200g small shallots, halved if large

2 tbsp brandy

750ml white wine

3 bay leaves

½ bunch of fresh thyme

500ml good-quality chicken stock

2 tsp cornflour (optional)

½ bunch of fresh flat-leaf parsley, leaves chopped

1. Preheat the oven to 180°C/160°C fan/gas 4.

2. Heat 2 tablespoons of the duck fat or butter in a large frying pan over high heat and, when hot, add the celery, onion and carrots and cook for 10 minutes, or until softened. Add the garlic and fry for another minute or two. Remove from the pan and set aside in an ovenproof casserole dish.

3. Combine the flour, salt and pepper, then dust the chicken pieces all over with the seasoned flour. Add the remaining 2 tablespoons of duck fat to the frying pan and fry the chicken pieces in batches until golden brown – each batch should take about 10 minutes. Remove from the pan and add to the casserole dish.

4. Add the bacon, mushrooms and shallots to the pan and fry for 5–7 minutes until well browned, then add to the chicken in the casserole dish.

5. Deglaze the pan with the brandy then pour this over the ingredients in the casserole dish. Place the casserole dish over the heat, add the wine, bay leaves and thyme (tied together with string) and bring to the boil. Simmer rapidly for about 15 minutes, then add the chicken stock and simmer gently for a further 15 minutes.

6. Cover and place in the oven for 40–50 minutes, or until the juices run clear when a chicken thigh is pierced with a knife in the thickest part. Remove the herbs tied with string. If you prefer a thicker sauce, mix the cornflour with a little water and stir into the sauce to thicken. Stir in the parsley and serve.

Chicken Chasseur

Chicken Chasseur isn't a million miles away from coq au vin in terms of the ingredients used. The key difference is tomatoes and they change everything, making the sauce more sweet and tangy. It's rich, flavourful and a really simple family-friendly recipe. I like to use a whole chicken and portion it up myself – it's an economical way to buy chicken and it leaves you with a carcass you can keep in the freezer for the next time you're making a stock or a gravy. However, this also works well with bone in chicken thighs and drumsticks.

SERVES: 4
PREP TIME: 20 MINUTES
COOKING TIME: ABOUT 1 HOUR

1 whole chicken (approx. 1.4kg),
cut into 8 pieces (or a mix of
8 chicken thighs and drumsticks)

3 tbsp plain flour

2 tbsp olive oil

1 tbsp butter

150g smoked bacon lardons

200g baby chestnut or button
mushrooms, halved if large

2 garlic cloves, crushed

250g shallots, halved if large

2 tsp caster sugar

2 tbsp brandy

1 tbsp tomato purée

175ml white wine

300ml good-quality chicken stock

3 large fresh tomatoes, skinned,
deseeded and chopped

4 tbsp chopped fresh tarragon

sea salt and freshly
ground black pepper

creamy mashed potato or Pomme
Mousseline (page 79), to serve

1. Preheat the oven to 180°C/160°C fan/gas 4. Place the chicken pieces on a plate, season all over with salt and pepper, then roll in the flour. Shake off and discard any excess flour.

2. Heat a large sauté pan until hot, add the oil and fry the chicken pieces, skin side down, for 2–3 minutes until golden-brown. Turn the chicken and fry on the other side for another 1–2 minutes, or until golden all over. Transfer the chicken pieces to an ovenproof casserole dish.

3. Now add the butter to the pan and fry the bacon and mushrooms until golden brown. Add the garlic and fry for another minute. Remove from the pan and transfer to the casserole dish. Add the shallots to the pan, sprinkle over the caster sugar and fry for 3–4 minutes, or until they are golden all over. Add the brandy and deglaze the pan over medium heat for 1–2 minutes, then add to the casserole dish with the chicken.

4. Place the casserole over medium heat, add the tomato purée and wine and bring to a simmer for a few minutes. Pour in the stock, tomatoes and half the tarragon and bring to the boil.

5. Cover with a lid and then cook in the preheated oven for 30–40 minutes, or until the chicken is cooked through and the sauce has thickened slightly. Remove from the oven and place on the hob over medium heat and cook for a few minutes to reduce the sauce, or until the sauce is the desired consistency.

6. Serve hot with creamy mashed potatoes or Pomme Mousseline and the remaining chopped tarragon scattered over.

French Onion Stew with Cheesy Thyme Croutons

This is my homage to one of the most famous French recipes in the world, onion soup. Classically served with slices of bread on top that are loaded with oozingly delicious melted cheese, it's no wonder that it's so popular! This version is somewhere between a soup and a stew and makes the most incredible side dish to accompany pork chops or sausages for something a little bit different and exciting. Don't worry, it's still got the cheesy croutons!

SERVES: 6 AS A SIDE DISH
PREP TIME: 15–20 MINUTES
COOKING TIME: ABOUT 1 HOUR

2 tbsp olive oil

knob of butter

4 large onions, thinly sliced

6 garlic cloves, crushed

2 bay leaves

2–3 sprigs of fresh thyme

1 tbsp soft dark brown sugar

1 tbsp red wine vinegar

2 heaped tbsp (30g) plain flour

250ml good-quality red wine

600ml strong beef stock

sea salt and freshly ground black pepper

handful of fresh thyme leaves, to finish

FOR THE CROUTONS

1 tbsp Dijon mustard

2 heaped tbsp crème fraîche

1 egg, beaten

1 tbsp chopped fresh thyme leaves

125g Comté or Gruyère cheese, finely grated

½ baguette, cut into 6 slices on the diagonal

1. Start by cooking the onions: heat the oil and butter in a deep, wide sauté pan or saucepan. Add the onions, garlic, bay leaves and thyme sprigs and cook over medium-low heat for 10–15 minutes, stirring frequently, until softened. Add the dark brown sugar and vinegar and continue cooking for a further 15–20 minutes until caramelised and dark golden brown and full of flavour, taking care not to let them catch and burn.

2. Add the flour to the pan, stir well and cook for a minute or two. Pour in the wine and allow to reduce by half, then add the stock and bring to the boil. Reduce the heat and simmer for a final 15 minutes, then season to taste with salt and pepper. The consistency should be somewhere between a soup and a stew. Remove and discard the bay leaves and thyme sprigs.

3. For the croutons, mix the Dijon mustard, crème fraîche, beaten egg, thyme leaves and cheese in a bowl until combined and season with salt and pepper.

4. Preheat the grill to high.

5. Arrange the baguette slices on a baking sheet and toast under the grill on one side for a minute or two, or until lightly golden. Turn over and spread the cheese mixture evenly over the slices. Return to the grill and grill for 2–3 minutes until the cheese has melted and is golden brown and bubbling.

6. To serve, pour the onion 'stew' into a large serving dish (approx. 1.5 litre capacity). Top with the cheesy croutons and sprinkle with thyme to finish. Serve as a side dish to sausages or pork chops.

Beef Fillet Bourguignon

Beef Bourguignon is not dissimilar to a coq au vin; it's a hearty casserole with bacon, mushrooms and wine at the base of its sauce. And like a classic coq au vin it can take a while to prepare. But the thing I love most about a bourguignon is the sauce itself, so with this recipe I've created a rich and delicious bourguignon style sauce to serve with steak or in this case roasted fillet of beef. This is a real savoury showstopper.

SERVES: 4
PREP TIME: 25 MINUTES
COOKING TIME: ABOUT 1 HOUR

FOR THE BEEF
1 tbsp olive oil
750–800g middle cut fillet of beef
sea salt and freshly ground black pepper

FOR THE SAUCE
1 tbsp olive oil
12 shallots, peeled but left whole
1 onion, thinly sliced
200g chestnut mushrooms, quartered
100g smoked back bacon, cut into 1cm chunks
½ fennel bulb, cut into 1cm dice
2 garlic cloves, finely grated
few sprigs of fresh thyme, leaves picked
2 bay leaves
1 tbsp plain flour
300ml red wine
100ml ruby port
300ml good-quality beef stock
1 tbsp chopped fresh tarragon (optional)

1. Preheat the oven to 200°C/180°C fan/gas 6.

2. Heat a large, high-sided sauté pan over high heat until it is very hot. Drizzle the beef fillet all over with the oil and season well with salt and pepper. Sear on all sides in the hot pan until golden all over – this should take just a couple of minutes. Transfer to a small roasting tray and then roast in the oven for 18 minutes for medium rare.

3. Meanwhile, make the sauce. Heat the olive oil in the same pan you used to sear the beef, add the whole shallots and fry for a few minutes until golden. Remove from the pan and set aside. Add the onion, mushrooms, bacon pieces and fennel and fry for 7–10 minutes, stirring frequently, until soft and golden. Add the garlic, thyme and the bay leaves and cook for a further 3 minutes. Season well with salt and pepper.

4. Remove the beef from the oven, cover lightly with foil and leave to rest while you continue with the sauce.

5. Return the shallots to the pan, add the flour and cook, stirring, for 1–2 minutes. Add the wine and port and bring to a simmer, scraping up all the flavourful bits from the bottom of the dish with a wooden spoon. After about 10 minutes the alcohol should have reduced to a syrup; at this point, add the beef stock and simmer over medium heat for 20 minutes, or until the sauce has thickened and reduced slightly. Stir in any juices from the rested fillet.

6. Thinly slice the rested beef and serve with the sauce. Finish by scattering over some chopped tarragon (if using).

Torte de Gibier with Madeira and Truffle Sauce

This is a recipe I learned when I was working at Michel Roux Jnr's incredible three-star Michelin restaurant, Le Gavroche. It was on the menu there for years and was, in my opinion, one of the most delicious things to come out of that kitchen. Gibier is the French word for game and the torte is a small pie made with puff pastry, encapsulating an amazing combination of game meats. Pork mince helps to balance out the strong flavour of game and the truffle sauce is sublime. Photographed overleaf.

SERVES: 4
PREP TIME: 40–45 MINUTES,
PLUS 1 HOUR 25 MINUTES CHILLING
COOKING TIME: ABOUT 35 MINUTES

FOR THE FILLING

200g pork mince

200g venison, finely chopped into 5mm pieces

200g game mix such as wood pigeon breast, pheasant and rabbit meat, finely chopped into 5mm pieces

2 garlic cloves, crushed

1 tbsp finely chopped fresh thyme leaves

1 tbsp chopped fresh sage

1 tbsp chopped fresh oregano

finely grated nutmeg

sea salt and freshly ground black pepper

FOR THE PASTRY

approx. 800g shop-bought all-butter puff pastry

plain flour, for dusting

2 tsp Dijon mustard

finely grated nutmeg

1 egg, beaten

1. To make the filling, put the pork mince, venison, game, garlic, thyme, sage and oregano into a large bowl. Season generously with salt and pepper and a good grating of nutmeg. Using your hands, mix well to combine. Divide into four tennis ball-sized balls, place on a tray, flatten a little and chill in the fridge for 30 minutes while you prepare the pastry.

2. Roll out the puff pastry on a lightly floured work surface until it is 3–5mm thick. Using a small plate (or bowl or large cutter), stamp out 4 × 13cm circles from one of the puff pastry sheets. Cut out another 4 × 15cm discs with the second sheet. You will have leftover pastry. Chill the discs in the fridge for 10–15 minutes to firm up. The small circles will be the base and the larger ones will act as the lid.

3. Arrange the smaller circles of pastry on a tray lined with baking parchment. Using a pastry brush, glaze each with some Dijon mustard and finely grate over a little dusting of nutmeg. Arrange a filling ball in the centre of each disc, then place the large disc of pastry on top of the filling and gently press down to flatten a little. Lightly press the pastry together, using the side of your hand, ensuring there are no air pockets and sealing the two pieces of pastry together at the base. Using a small knife, trim the edges to make a neat circle, then use a fork to crimp the edges. Glaze the pie by brushing with the beaten egg and cut a small slit in the top. Return to the fridge to chill for 30 minutes.

4. Preheat the oven to 220°C/200°C fan/gas 7. Place a large flat baking sheet in the oven to heat up.

Continued Overleaf …

FOR THE SAUCE
knob of butter
1 tbsp olive oil
2 banana shallots, finely chopped
2 garlic cloves, crushed
250ml Madeira
6 juniper berries, finely ground with pestle and mortar
250ml red wine
400ml good-quality chicken stock
2 tsp finely chopped truffle (in oil)

5. Once chilled, repeat the egg wash process and glaze each pie all over. Score each one using a small sharp knife: starting from the centre, create fine spiral lines going outwards down to the edges, roughly 1cm apart. Chill again for another 10 minutes.

6. Carefully transfer the chilled pies on their sheet of parchment directly onto the hot baking sheet in the oven and cook for 20 minutes. Reduce the oven temperature to 200°C/180°C fan/gas 6 and cook for a further 10–15 minutes, until risen and golden brown.

7. Meanwhile, make the sauce. Heat the butter and oil in a medium saucepan or sauté pan. Add the shallots and cook for 6–8 minutes over medium-low heat until softened. Stir in the garlic and cook for a further 2 minutes. Pour in the Madeira, add the juniper berries and allow to reduce over high heat for a further 4–5 minutes. Add the red wine and again reduce by half (this should take 5–6 minutes). Pour in the stock, reduce the heat and simmer for about 15 minutes until thickened. Drain the chopped truffle from the oil and stir into the sauce. Season to taste.

8. Remove the pies from the oven, transfer to serving plates and serve with the truffle sauce.

Potatoes Three Ways

If there's one vegetable that the French have absolutely mastered cooking, it's the humble potato. So much so that there's not one, but three classic recipes that I knew I had to include in this chapter. Pommes Mousseline is France's answer to mashed potatoes and is absolutely sublime – there's no scrimping on the butter or cream. Dauphinoise make for a really special alternative to roasties with a Sunday lunch and Pommes Lyonnaise – thinly sliced potatoes fried with onions – are an amazing accompaniment for any meat or fish dish.

Dauphinoise Potatoes

SERVES: 6–8
PREP TIME: 30 MINUTES
COOKING TIME: ABOUT 2 HOURS

butter, for greasing

2 tbsp olive oil

2 large onions, thinly sliced

4 garlic cloves, thinly sliced

1.2kg floury potatoes (such as Maris Piper), peeled

4–6 sprigs of fresh thyme, leaves picked

500ml double cream

2 tsp Dijon mustard (optional)

¼ tsp freshly grated nutmeg

200ml milk

100g crème fraîche (optional)

100g Gruyère cheese, grated

sea salt and freshly ground black pepper

1. Preheat the oven to 180°C/160°C fan/gas 4. Grease a large ovenproof dish (32 × 20cm, approx. 2 litre capacity) with butter.

2. Heat the oil in a large non-stick frying pan and sauté the onions with a good pinch of salt and pepper for 8–10 minutes until softened. Stir in the garlic and cook for a further couple of minutes. Remove from the heat and set aside.

3. Using a mandoline (or a food processor with a slicer attachment), thinly slice the potatoes to a thickness of around 1–2mm.

4. Arrange a layer of potato slices in the base of the prepared oven dish and season with a little salt and pepper. Follow with a thin layer of cooked onion and garlic and scatter over some picked thyme leaves. Repeat with a layer of potatoes, seasoning, onions and thyme, layering until they have all been used, finishing with a final layer of potatoes neatly arranged on top.

5. Place the cream in a large jug and whisk in the Dijon mustard (if using), grated nutmeg, milk and crème fraîche (if using) and pour over the potatoes, making sure they are covered. Press down gently and allow to absorb into the potatoes.

6. Cover the dish with foil and bake the dauphinoise in the oven for 1¼–1½ hours – insert a knife into the centre to check that the potatoes are tender and soft. Remove from the oven, discard the foil and increase the oven temperature to 200°C/180°C/gas 6.

7. Sprinkle the top of the dauphinoise evenly with the grated cheese and return to the oven for 15–20 minutes until golden brown and bubbling. Allow to sit for 10 minutes before serving.

Pommes Lyonnaise

SERVES: 4–6
PREP TIME: 10–15 MINUTES
COOKING TIME: 45–50 MINUTES

1kg Desiree potatoes, scrubbed

3 tbsp olive oil or duck fat

2 sweet white onions, thinly sliced

3 sprigs of fresh thyme, leaves picked

3 garlic cloves, thinly sliced

50g butter

2 tbsp chopped fresh flat-leaf parsley

sea salt and freshly ground black pepper

1. Leaving the skins on, thinly slice the potatoes into 3mm slices. Bring a large saucepan of boiling salted water to the boil, add the potato slices and cook for 5 minutes, or until just tender but not falling apart. Drain carefully and set aside to steam dry for a few minutes.

2. Meanwhile, in a large sauté pan melt 1 tablespoon of the olive oil or duck fat, add the onions and thyme leaves, season well and fry over medium-low heat for about 15 minutes, stirring frequently, until the onions have softened and turned golden brown. Add the sliced garlic and fry for another 2–3 minutes. Remove from the pan and set aside.

3. Melt a quarter of the butter and ½ tablespoon of duck fat or olive oil in the same pan, add a quarter of the potatoes and season well. Fry over medium heat until they are golden on both sides. Tip into a dish and keep warm while you repeat until all the potatoes are cooked.

4. To serve, pile the fried potatoes into a serving dish, scatter the golden onions over the top and sprinkle with the parsley.

Pommes Mousseline

SERVES: 4–6
PREP TIME: 20 MINUTES
COOKING TIME: ABOUT 40 MINUTES

650g waxy potatoes (such as
Charlotte), peeled

200ml milk

200ml double cream

50g cold butter, diced

sea salt and freshly ground black
pepper

1. Put the potatoes into a saucepan and cover with cold water. Add a good pinch of salt, cover and bring to the boil. Then turn the heat down and simmer gently – don't boil them – for about 30 minutes until the potatoes feel soft when gently squeezed. Remove from the heat.

2. One at a time, use a slotted spoon to take the potatoes out of the water and, wearing clean rubber gloves (as they'll be very hot), peel off the skin with a small sharp knife. As soon as they're all peeled, work them through a sieve (or use a food mill or mouli if you have one). Be careful not to scrape or drag the potatoes across the sieve so that they don't turn gluey.

3. Tip the puréed potatoes into a clean pan. Bring the milk and cream to boiling point in another pan, then remove from the heat. Using a rubber spatula, beat a third of the creamy milk into the potatoes over medium heat, followed by a third of the diced butter.

4. Carry on beating in the milk and butter in two more batches. The potatoes will become shiny and silky smooth. Make sure each batch of milk and butter is fully incorporated before adding the next, and switch to a balloon whisk when the purée gets to the liquid stage. The purée should be as smooth as silk after adding all the hot creamy milk and butter, and quite runny. Season to taste before serving.

Lavender Peach Melba

Anyone who knows me knows I am obsessed with lavender! There are very few recipes I won't try to sneak it into, so when I was coming up with a twist on a classic peach melba, I knew it had to involve lavender. The traditional recipe was invented by renowned French chef Auguste Escoffier in the late 1800s and combines peaches and raspberries. They're a perfect pairing, beautifully enhanced by the addition of my favourite flower.

SERVES: 4
PREP TIME: 10 MINUTES
COOKING TIME: ABOUT 30 MINUTES
PLUS COOLING

FOR THE PEACHES
500ml cold water

200g caster sugar

2 tbsp lavender flowers

1 cinnamon stick

1 lemon, skin peeled into strips

4 ripe peaches, halved and stones removed

FOR THE RASPBERRY SAUCE
200g raspberries

1 tbsp caster sugar

1 vanilla pod, halved lengthways and seeds scraped out

2 tbsp Chambord

TO SERVE
crème fraîche or vanilla ice cream

25g flaked almonds, toasted

lavender flowers, to decorate

1. Start by poaching the peaches. Pour the water into a large saucepan. Add the caster sugar, lavender flowers, cinnamon stick and lemon peel. Bring to the boil, then reduce the heat to a low simmer and cook for 5 minutes, stirring to dissolve the sugar. Add the peach halves and poach gently for 10–12 minutes until the peaches are tender.

2. Turn the heat off and allow the peaches to cool and infuse in the flavoured syrup. Once cool enough to handle, remove from the syrup, peel off the skins and set aside.

3. To make the raspberry sauce, heat the raspberries, sugar, vanilla seeds and Chambord together in a medium saucepan. Cook for 5–6 minutes, stirring to dissolve the sugar, until the raspberries have turned to a pulp. Remove from the heat and strain through a sieve into a jug.

4. To serve, place a scoop of ice cream or crème fraîche onto serving plates alongside the two peach halves and a little of the syrup. Drizzle over some raspberry sauce and sprinkle with flaked almonds and a few lavender flowers to serve.

MARCUS'S TIPS

If you have any poaching syrup left over, strain it to remove the spices and vanilla pod then store it in a jar to use in cocktails or drizzled over vanilla ice cream for another easy sweet treat.
If you're short of time you can make a speedy version of this recipe using tinned peaches instead of poaching your own.

Apple Tarte Tatin with Nutmeg Cream

My first ever attempt at making an apple tarte tatin was in a competition at The Savoy hotel in London – talk about being thrown in at the deep end! It did not go well. I had no idea that the apples needed to be caramelised, which I soon realised is the key to a perfect tarte tatin. I'm happy to say that I've mastered the technique since then and this recipe is both foolproof and delicious. Photographed overleaf.

SERVES: 6–8
PREP TIME: 20 MINUTES
COOKING TIME: ABOUT 50 MINUTES

1 x 320g sheet of ready-rolled all-butter puff pastry

plain flour, for dusting

100g cold butter, softened

100g golden caster sugar

2 cardamon pods, bashed gently with a rolling pin to release the flavour

1 cinnamon stick

6–7 Braeburn apples, peeled and quartered

FOR THE NUTMEG CREAM
200ml double or whipping cream

a grating of fresh nutmeg

1. To make the tarte tatin, roll out the puff pastry on a floured work surface to about 3mm thick and cut around a plate to make a large circle, just bigger than the pan you're going to use to make the tart. Cut three small slits in the pastry for the steam to escape and move to a baking parchment-lined tray. Place in the fridge to rest while you make the rest of the tart.

2. Spread the softened butter in an even layer over the base of a 20–24cm ovenproof frying pan. Cover with the sugar and spices in another even layer. Arrange the apples on top in a spiral, overlapping one another.

3. Preheat the oven to 210°C/190°C fan/gas 7.

4. Place the pan on the hob over medium-high heat and cook until the butter and sugar start to form a caramel; this will take around 10 minutes. Remove from the heat and then place the pastry circle over the apples, using a spoon to tuck the pastry in around the edges of the pan. Be careful; it will be very hot!

5. Bake for about 35–40 minutes until golden brown. Remove from the oven and leave to rest for 5 minutes.

6. Meanwhile, make the nutmeg cream by whisking the cream until it forms soft peaks. Spoon into a serving bowl and grate some fresh nutmeg over the top.

7. Run a small knife around the inside of the pan to ease away the caramelised pastry. Put a large plate over the tarte tatin in the pan and carefully flip both pan and plate over. Slowly lift the pan off to turn the tarte out. Serve with the nutmeg cream on the side.

Gooseberry, Elderflower and Rosemary Bavarois with Almond Praline

A bavarois is essentially a set custard dessert. A vanilla – and in this recipe, rosemary – infused crème anglaise is combined with whipped cream and gelatine and then set in the fridge and served chilled. I've also added a gooseberry purée to mine, which is sharp, tangy and flavoured with the delicate floral notes of elderflower. The result is a smooth, creamy and beautiful-tasting dessert that's perfectly topped off with sweet and crunchy almond praline. Photographed overleaf.

SERVES: 8
PREP TIME: 25–30 MINUTES
COOKING TIME: ABOUT 20 MINUTES,
PLUS 4–5 HOURS FOR COOLING

FOR THE GOOSEBERRY PURÉE
500g fresh or frozen gooseberries

125g caster sugar

2 tbsp elderflower cordial (or liquor)

1 vanilla pod, halved lengthways
and seeds scraped out

grated zest and juice of 1 lemon

FOR THE BAVAROIS
250ml milk

450ml double cream

1 vanilla pod, halved

2 sprigs of fresh rosemary

3 sheets of gelatine

6 egg yolks

100g caster sugar

1. Start by making the gooseberry purée. Put the gooseberries, caster sugar, elderflower cordial, vanilla seeds and lemon zest and juice into a large saucepan and heat over low-medium heat for 8–10 minutes, stirring occasionally, until the gooseberries have broken down and are softened.

2. Transfer to a blender or food processor and blitz until smooth, then set aside and leave to cool completely.

3. To make the bavarois, heat the milk, 250ml of the double cream, the vanilla pod and rosemary sprigs in a medium saucepan almost to boiling point. Turn off the heat and allow to cool for 5 minutes. Meanwhile, soak the gelatine sheets in a bowl of cold water for 3–5 minutes, then squeeze the water out of the gelatine sheets, add them to the infused milk and cream mixture and stir until dissolved. Allow to infuse for around 20–30 minutes, then strain into a jug and discard the vanilla and rosemary sprigs.

4. Whisk the egg yolks and sugar in a medium bowl until pale and thickened. Gradually whisk in the infused milk and cream, stirring to combine, then return to the pan and warm gently, stirring continuously until thickened and the mixture coats the back of a spoon. Take care not to boil the bavarois as the egg yolks will scramble. Transfer to a bowl and place a circle of baking parchment directly on top, to prevent a skin from forming. Set aside to cool for around an hour.

FOR THE ALMOND PRALINE

75g caster sugar

100g whole blanched almonds, toasted and roughly chopped

5. Once everything has cooled, whip the remaining 200ml double cream in a large bowl to soft peaks. Gently fold the cream through the custard to combine, then add the gooseberry purée and fold again gently to combine.

6. Spoon into eight glass dishes (approx. 150–200ml) and chill in the fridge for 2–3 hours, or until set.

7. To make the praline, heat the sugar and 2 tablespoons of water in a stainless-steel saucepan until dissolved, and starting to turn a dark amber colour. Remove from the heat and immediately add the almonds, swirling to evenly coat. Carefully tip out onto a baking tray lined with baking parchment and leave to cool completely.

8. Finely chop up or break the praline into little pieces and scatter over the gooseberry bavarois in a thin layer to make a crunchy topping. Serve.

MARCUS'S TIP

If gooseberries aren't your thing, you can switch them out for other berries of your choice. Blackcurrants would work especially well as they're more on the sharp side, like gooseberries.

Cooking

Over Fire

Writing this chapter has taken me right back to the year I turned 21, when Albert Roux sent me to cook in Upstate New York and I mastered the art of the grill. The first thing I want to say about cooking over fire is that there's much more to it than you might think. There are so many ways to cook with a simple barbecue and I use a few different methods in this chapter. The key is to think of your barbecue like the stove in your kitchen. So you can put pans on the grate as you would on the hob (as long as they don't have plastic handles!). And you can use the lid to create an oven-like environment inside your barbecue. Another thing I often tell people is that if you can get yourself a barbecue with a raised section, this will completely change the way you cook over fire. A raised grill is where you can set your meat to rest or even to slow-cook away from the intensity of the direct heat, a bit like you would in a low oven. It turns a simple barbecue into something quite versatile. But there's one thing that anyone can do, regardless of the type of barbecue you have, and that's to cook certain ingredients right on the coals. This is an amazing way to roast root vegetables and potatoes wrapped in foil or to char the skin of peppers and onions for a smoky salsa.

In this chapter I hope to encourage you to experiment and get comfortable with some of these methods to take your barbecue game to a whole new level.

Barbecued Prawns with Garlic, Chilli and Lemon Butter

Smoky Aubergine and Garlic Dip with Pitta 'Chips'

Barbecued Chicory with Baked Goats' Cheese,
Fig Jam and Orange and Mustard Dressing

Honeyed Carrots with Crème Fraîche
and Hazelnuts

Whole Barbecued Sea Bream with Rosemary Potatoes
and a Shallot, Caper and Parsley Vinaigrette

The Ultimate Steak Sandwich

Sticky Barbecue Pork Loin with Herby Green Sauce

Pork Skewers with Fennel and Apple Slaw
and a Smoky Garlic and Paprika Dip

Spiced Barbecued Corn on the Cob

Lamb Ribs with Sweet Calvados Glaze

Rib of Beef with Provençal Beans

Charred Leeks with Roasted Red Pepper
and Anchovy Dressing

Barbecued Piquant Red Pepper Spatchcock Chicken

Brie-topped Burger with Mustard Mayonnaise
and Grilled Potato Wedges

Barbecued Fruits with Toasted Oat Crumble
and Whipped Crème Fraîche

Barbecued Prawns with Garlic, Chilli and Lemon Butter

Prawns are absolutely fabulous on the barbecue: they're simple to prepare, quick to cook and look impressive too. Pour over a sizzling hot garlic butter, toast some baguette slices to dip into the juices and prepare to get messy! These are great as part of a big barbecue spread, but they're also a wonderful lunch all on their own. I recommend having a few bowls of lemon water dotted around to wash your fingers.

SERVES: 4 AS A STARTER
PREP TIME: 10 MINUTES
COOKING TIME: ABOUT 10 MINUTES

FOR THE BARBECUED PRAWNS
24 whole raw prawns

6 tbsp olive oil

sea salt and freshly ground black pepper

lemon wedges, to serve

FOR THE TOASTS
olive oil

1 small baguette, cut into 8 slices on the diagonal

FOR THE GARLIC BUTTER
100g butter

8 garlic cloves, crushed

1 red chilli, deseeded and finely chopped

small handful of fresh flat-leaf parsley, chopped

grated zest of 1 lemon

1. Light the barbecue; it is ready when the flames have died down and the embers are glowing.

2. Place the prawns in a large bowl, pour over the olive oil and season well with salt and pepper.

3. For the toasts, drizzle olive oil over each side of the bread and season with salt and pepper.

4. Add the prawns to the hot grate and cook for 2–3 minutes on each side until bright pink and cooked through. Transfer to a serving platter.

5. Add the bread slices to the grate and cook for 1–2 minutes on each side until charred and crisp. Grill the lemon wedges, if liked.

6. Meanwhile, heat a cast-iron pan on the barbecue and add the butter. Once melted, add the crushed garlic, chilli, parsley and lemon zest. Season with salt and pepper and cook for 1–2 minutes while stirring.

7. Pour the sizzling garlic butter over the cooked prawns and serve immediately with lemon wedges to squeeze over and the crusty toasts to mop up all the juices.

MARCUS'S TIP

If you've made a batch of the herbed garlic compound butter on page 33, that would also work well on these prawns.

Smoky Aubergine and Garlic Dip with Pitta 'Chips'

Cooking aubergines directly on the coals of a barbecue gives them the most incredible smoky flavour; doing the same with a whole bulb of garlic takes away its harshness, making this dip utterly delicious. The herby pitta 'chips' are my answer to melba toasts, which, like peach melba, were invented by Auguste Escoffier at The Savoy hotel for a guest who wanted their toast to be extra dry. They're crispy, crunchy and perfect for dipping.

SERVES: 4
PREP TIME: 10–15 MINUTES
COOKING TIME: 35 MINUTES

FOR THE AUBERGINE AND GARLIC DIP
2 large aubergines

1 whole garlic bulb

grated zest of ½ lemon, plus a squeeze of juice

2 tbsp tahini

2 tbsp natural yoghurt

1 tsp finely chopped fresh thyme leaves

sea salt and freshly ground black pepper

FOR THE PITTA 'CHIPS'
4 pitta breads

olive oil

2 tsp herbes de Provence

TO SERVE
extra virgin olive oil

paprika

grated lemon zest

1. Light the barbecue; it is ready when the flames have died down and the embers are glowing.

2. Add the whole aubergines and garlic bulb directly to the coals and cook for 20–25 minutes, using tongs to turn frequently, until the aubergine skins have split, are charred evenly and both the aubergines and garlic are softened. Remove from the heat, sit the aubergines in a colander over a bowl to release the excess liquid and allow to cool.

3. Prepare the pitta 'chips' – drizzle each bread with a good glug of olive oil and sprinkle with herbes de Provence. Season well with salt and pepper, place on the hot grate and toast for 2 minutes on each side until golden brown. Remove from the heat and cut into thick strips on the diagonal to resemble chunky chips.

4. Once the aubergine is cool enough to handle, peel back the burnt skin and discard. Cut in half lengthways, then roughly chop the aubergine flesh and add to a large bowl. Remove the garlic pulp from the bulb by squeezing out the skins into the bowl and mash together with the aubergine. Add the lemon zest and a squeeze of juice, tahini, yoghurt, thyme and season well with salt and pepper to taste.

5. To serve, spoon the smoky aubergine dip into a serving bowl and top with a drizzle of extra virgin olive oil, a sprinkle of paprika and a little lemon zest. Serve the pitta 'chips' alongside.

Barbecued Chicory with Baked Goats' Cheese, Fig Jam and Orange and Mustard Dressing

Goats' cheese salad is something you will see on menus all over France; it's a simple but delicious recipe that I've eaten and enjoyed countless times. I wanted to create my own version cooked on the barbecue to bring a different taste to this classic salad. The goats' cheese stuffed with fig jam is a revelation and the flavour that the fire brings to the chicory and other salad vegetables makes this a really special dish. Photographed overleaf.

SERVES: 4
PREP TIME: 15–20 MINUTES
COOKING TIME: 15–20 MINUTES

FOR THE SALAD
2 heads of red chicory

2 heads of white chicory

4 spring onions

4 figs, cut in half

2 baby gem lettuce

4 tbsp olive oil

juice of ½ orange

sea salt and freshly ground black pepper

FOR THE BAKED GOATS' CHEESE
4 small goats' cheese rounds (such as crottin de chèvre) or 2 x 100g goats' cheese rounds, halved horizontally

2 tbsp fig jam

olive oil

2 sprigs of fresh thyme, leaves picked

1. Light the barbecue; it is ready when the flames have died down and the embers are glowing.

2. Cut the red and white chicory in half lengthways. Trim the spring onions so that they are a similar length to the chicory heads but leave the roots intact. Add both to a large bowl with the halved figs. Cut the baby gem in half lengthways and then in half again to make long wedges; add these to the bowl. Drizzle in the olive oil and a generous pinch of seasoning, then add the orange juice and gently toss together to coat.

3. Chargrill the chicory, spring onions and baby gem quarters on the hot barbecue for 8–10 minutes, turning frequently until evenly charred and tender. Add the figs for the last few minutes of cooking. Move them around the barbecue if some spots are hotter than others. Remove from the heat and cut the chicory in half lengthways to make long wedges.

4. For the baked goats' cheese – arrange the individual goats' cheeses (or rounds) into a small cast-iron skillet (or non-stick frying pan). Make a little hole in the centre of each cheese and spoon the fig jam inside, pushing it down into the centre. Drizzle with olive oil, season with salt and pepper and scatter with the thyme leaves. Place on the barbecue, cover with the lid and cook for 4–5 minutes, so the cheese is just starting to melt, but still holding its shape. Keep an eye on it and move away from the direct heat if it's too fierce.

Continued Overleaf …

FOR THE TOASTS
4 slices of baguette, cut on the
diagonal
olive oil
1 garlic clove, halved

FOR THE DRESSING
2 tsp wholegrain mustard
1 tsp Dijon mustard
1 tsp orange blossom honey
1 tbsp red wine vinegar
grated zest and juice of ½ orange
50ml extra virgin olive oil

5. For the toasts, drizzle the baguette slices with olive oil and season. Toast on the hot barbecue for 1–2 minutes on each side, until charred and golden. Remove from the heat and lightly rub with the cut side of the garlic clove.

6. To make the dressing, whisk the mustards, honey and red wine vinegar together in a small bowl to combine. Add the orange zest and juice and gradually whisk in the extra virgin olive oil until combined. Season with salt and pepper.

7. To serve, divide the charred chicory, spring onions, baby gem and figs among serving plates. Arrange the baked goats' cheese and jammy fig mixture on top. Place the garlic toasts alongside and drizzle with a little orange dressing to serve. Serve any remaining dressing alongside.

MARCUS'S TIP

When it's in season, asparagus makes a fantastic addition to this salad. Simply add a handful of spears to the bowl with the chicory, lettuce and spring onions and cook as you would the rest of the veg. If you struggle to find fig jam you can swap it for apricot jam or any type of chutney that goes with cheese, such as red onion or gooseberry.

Honeyed Carrots with Crème Fraîche and Hazelnuts

This is one of my favourite ways to cook carrots, turning this humble vegetable into something really special. Whether you're having a quiet family barbecue or are celebrating a special occasion with an outdoor dinner party, this is the perfect vegetable side dish. Honey enhances the natural sweetness of the carrots and that is perfectly balanced by the crème fraîche and tangy dressing. The toasted hazelnuts add crunch and depth of flavour while the herbs bring colour and freshness.

SERVES: 4 AS A SIDE DISH
PREP TIME: 15 MINUTES
COOKING TIME: ABOUT 30 MINUTES

500g bunch of carrots (heritage if possible), halved lengthways

1 tsp cumin seeds, toasted

2 tbsp olive oil

2 tbsp honey

sea salt and freshly ground black pepper

FOR THE DRESSING
1 tsp Dijon mustard

1 tbsp white wine vinegar

50ml extra virgin olive oil

TO SERVE
20g hazelnuts

200g crème fraîche

handful of fresh chopped mixed soft herbs such as mint, chives, parsley or oregano

1. Light the barbecue; it is ready when the flames have died down and the embers are white.

2. Arrange the carrots on a double sheet of foil. Sprinkle with the cumin seeds, olive oil and honey and season with salt and pepper. Wrap the foil around the carrots to form a tight parcel, then carefully bury it in the coals. Cook for 20–30 minutes, turning the parcel regularly. The carrots are done when they are soft when poked with a knife. (To cook the carrots indoors, preheat the oven to 200°C/180°C fan/gas 6. Place all the ingredients on a baking tray lined with baking parchment and roast for 30 minutes, turning occasionally, or until tender and golden all over.)

3. To make the dressing, mix the mustard, vinegar and extra virgin olive oil in a small bowl and season with salt and pepper.

4. Toast the hazelnuts in a dry frying pan on the grate of the barbecue for 2–3 minutes, then roughly chop.

5. To serve, spread the crème fraîche over a platter and top with the carrots and their cooking juices. Drizzle over the dressing, then finish with the hazelnuts and any soft herbs you have to hand.

Whole Barbecued Sea Bream with Rosemary Potatoes and a Shallot, Caper and Parsley Vinaigrette

Whole fish cooked over fire cannot be beaten. It retains so much moisture when it's cooked on the bone and the flavour from the smoky barbecue and the charred skin is incredible. Cooking the potatoes in a pan on the barbecue grate ensures some of that smoky flavour gets in there too and topping it all off with a tangy, sweet and herby vinaigrette is just beautiful. If the French had invented fish and chips, I'm sure it would look like this. Photographed overleaf.

SERVES: 4
PREP TIME: 15–20 MINUTES
COOKING TIME: 30–35 MINUTES

FOR THE SEA BREAM
2 whole sea bream, scaled and gutted
olive oil
1 lemon, cut into slices
1 fennel bulb, thinly sliced
small bunch of fresh parsley stalks
sea salt and freshly ground black pepper

FOR THE POTATOES
400g baby potatoes, skin on and thickly sliced
1 banana shallot, thinly sliced
2 garlic cloves, peeled but left whole
2 sprigs of fresh rosemary

1. Light the barbecue; it is ready when the flames have died down and the embers are glowing.

2. Pat the fish dry using kitchen paper, then use a sharp knife to lightly score the fillets. Season the outside of the fish and the cavities with salt and pepper. Rub olive oil generously over the fish, then stuff the lemon and fennel slices and parsley stalks inside the cavities.

3. Place the fish on the hot barbecue grate and cook for 6–8 minutes, then carefully turn over the fish using a fish slice to prevent them sticking or breaking apart. Cook for a further 6–8 minutes until the flesh is opaque. Remove and set aside to keep warm.

4. For the potatoes, bring a large saucepan of salted water to the boil and cook the potatoes for 6–8 minutes until tender. Drain and allow to steam dry for 5 minutes. Heat a large cast-iron pan on the barbecue and drizzle with a good glug of olive oil. Add the shallot and cook for a couple of minutes until softened. Add the garlic cloves, cooked potatoes, rosemary sprigs and season with salt and pepper and cook for 8–10 minutes, turning frequently until the potatoes are golden brown and crispy.

FOR THE SHALLOT, CAPER AND PARSLEY VINAIGRETTE

2 small banana shallots, very finely diced

2 tbsp baby capers

75ml extra virgin olive oil

1 tbsp white wine vinegar

drizzle of honey

2 tbsp chopped fresh flat-leaf parsley

5. For the vinaigrette, place all the ingredients into a small bowl, season with salt and pepper and mix to combine.

6. Transfer the fish to a serving platter and arrange the rosemary potatoes alongside. Serve with the vinaigrette drizzled over the fish.

MARCUS'S TIP

Some people might be put off the idea of barbecuing whole fish for fear of the skin sticking to the grate, and the truth is, it's very hard to avoid. However, my tip is embrace the slightly torn and broken bits of skin, they always get extra crispy over the fire and are utterly delicious. They're part of the character of the dish. Although this recipe calls for sea bream, any small white fish will do, such as sea bass, or whatever is available to you that you enjoy eating.

The Ultimate Steak Sandwich

A great steak sandwich is a thing of beauty. You can add caramelised onions, blue cheese, bacon jam – really anything you like, but I'm keeping it simple and classic with this recipe. It's all about the rub for the steak; it brings amazing flavour and you can vary it depending on what herbs and spices you have in your store cupboard.

SERVES: 4
PREP TIME: 15 MINUTES
COOKING TIME: ABOUT 10 MINUTES

2 sirloin steaks, about 3cm thick

2 tbsp olive oil

1 tbsp salt

1 tsp dried chilli flakes

1 tsp smoked paprika

1 tsp crushed peppercorns

2 large ciabatta loaves

4 tbsp Dijon mustard

200g garden salad leaves (watercress or rocket both work well)

4 tbsp mayonnaise

1. Remove the steaks from the fridge at least half an hour before cooking to allow them to reach room temperature. Meanwhile, light the barbecue.

2. Score the fat on the steaks to prevent them from curling while cooking and rub all over with the olive oil. In a small bowl, combine the salt, chilli flakes, paprika and peppercorns and then rub this onto the steaks.

3. When the flames on the barbecue have died down and the embers are glowing, place the steaks onto the grate for 3 minutes on each side, or until cooked to your liking. (To cook indoors: sear the steaks in a hot pan for 3 minutes each side and then, if necessary, finish off in the oven at 200°C/180°C fan/gas 6 for a few minutes if they are still very rare after searing.)

4. Transfer the steaks to a board and allow to rest for 3 minutes before slicing.

5. Slice the ciabatta loaves in half lengthways and toast the cut sides on the grate for 2 minutes.

6. Once toasted, spread the ciabatta bases with the mustard and add a pile of garden salad leaves.

7. Thinly slice the steaks and place on top of the salad leaves. Dollop with mayonnaise, top with the ciabatta tops and cut into four sandwiches. Serve immediately.

MARCUS'S TIP

You can use whatever steak you like for a sandwich, but for me the best is a sirloin. It's got the perfect ratio of fat to meat to give it the most amazing texture.

Sticky Barbecue Pork Loin with Herby Green Sauce

If you want to shake things up at your next barbecue and try something other than the classic burgers and hot dogs we all know and love, this is the recipe for you. Soft brioche buns are filled with slices of succulent pork and a flavour-packed sauce inspired by my time spent in the south of France, where fresh herbs and capers are abundant. This has become a firm favourite in my house, and I hope it does in yours too.

SERVES: 4
PREP TIME: 20 MINUTES
COOKING TIME: ABOUT 10 MINUTES

1 tsp mustard powder

1 tsp smoked paprika

1 tsp chopped fresh rosemary leaves

2 tbsp soft dark brown sugar

2 tbsp cold-pressed rapeseed oil

500g pork loin, cut into 2.5cm-thick slices

sea salt and freshly ground pepper

4 brioche buns, halved, to serve

FOR THE HERBY GREEN SAUCE
1 small white onion, chopped

1 tbsp capers, drained

½ bunch of fresh flat-leaf parsley

½ bunch of fresh tarragon

½ bunch of fresh oregano

4 tbsp extra virgin olive oil

splash of white wine vinegar

FOR THE SLAW
1 Granny Smith apple

300g celeriac

2 tbsp Greek-style yoghurt

1 tsp Dijon mustard

1. Mix together the mustard, paprika, rosemary, sugar and oil. Rub generously all over the meat. Leave to marinate while you make the herby green sauce and slaw.

2. Make the herby green sauce by putting all the ingredients in a blender (including the stems of the herbs) and blending to a smooth paste. Season with salt and pepper, then set aside.

3. To make the slaw, peel the apple and celeriac and slice into thin matchsticks, then add to a bowl with the yoghurt and mustard and stir to combine. Set aside.

4. Light the barbecue; it is ready when the flames have died down and the embers are glowing. Place the marinated pork slices onto the hot grate and cook for 3 minutes on each side until cooked through. Leave to rest for 4 minutes then slice into smaller pieces. (To cook the pork loin indoors: place the pork slices onto a hot griddle pan and griddle for 3 minutes on each side, or until cooked through.)

5. Toast the cut sides of the buns on the grate. Load up the buns with the slaw, herby green sauce and sliced pork.

Pork Skewers with Fennel and Apple Slaw and a Smoky Garlic and Paprika Dip

Whenever I've been to a butcher or a market stall selling sausages in France, I've been blown away by the range of different types and flavours they have on offer. Back home, I like to buy pork mince and flavour it myself with various herbs and spices, and turn the mince into koftas which are amazing on the barbecue.

MAKES: 8 SKEWERS
PREP TIME: 35 MINUTES
COOKING TIME: 10–12 MINUTES

FOR THE PORK SKEWERS
500g pork mince (preferably 20% fat)
2 shallots, finely chopped
4 roasted garlic cloves, mashed
2 tsp fennel seeds, crushed
2 tbsp finely chopped fresh sage
2 tbsp finely chopped fresh oregano
sea salt and freshly ground black pepper
grated lemon zest, to finish

FOR THE SLAW
1 small fennel bulb, finely shredded
¼ red cabbage, finely shredded
1 shallot, finely shredded
1 apple, cored and finely shredded
4 tbsp mayonnaise
juice of ½ lemon
2 tsp wholegrain mustard
2 tbsp finely chopped fresh tarragon

FOR THE DIP
150g natural yoghurt
4 roasted garlic cloves, mashed
1 tsp smoked paprika
1 heaped tsp harissa paste (optional)

1. Light the barbecue; it is ready when the flames have died down and the embers are glowing.

2. Put the pork mince into a large bowl. Add the shallots, roasted garlic, fennel seeds, sage and oregano and season with salt and pepper. Mix together well to combine and mould into 8 kofta shapes with your hands. Thread each kofta onto a wooden skewer, pressing around to secure.

3. Cook the skewers on the hot barbecue grate for 10–12 minutes, turning frequently, until evenly browned and cooked through.

4. For the slaw, mix the fennel, cabbage, shallot and apple in a large bowl. Add the mayonnaise, lemon juice, mustard, tarragon and a good pinch of salt and pepper and mix to combine.

5. To make the dip, mix together the yoghurt, roasted garlic, paprika and a good pinch of salt and pepper. Ripple through the harissa (if using).

6. To serve, spoon the slaw onto serving plates. Top with pork skewers and serve a good dollop of the smoky dip alongside. Finish with a little lemon zest to serve.

MARCUS'S TIP

Soak your wooden skewers for 1 hour to make them less likely to burn.

Spiced Barbecued Corn on the Cob

Corn on the cob is one of our favourite vegetables to barbecue, but we don't tend to add much to it other than lashings of butter! This recipe not only has a spiced butter, but also a flavour-packed herby vinaigrette to really up the ante.

SERVES: 4 AS A SIDE DISH
PREP TIME: 15–20 MINUTES
COOKING TIME: 12–15 MINUTES

FOR THE CORN
4 corn on the cob, in husks

FOR THE SPICED BUTTER
100g soft butter
1 tbsp honey
¼ tsp cayenne pepper
sea salt

FOR THE HERB DRESSING
6 tbsp fresh chopped mixed soft herbs such as mint, basil, tarragon, parsley, chives, coriander or dill
1 banana shallot, chopped
1 tbsp capers, chopped
1 garlic clove, crushed
juice of ½ lemon
100ml olive oil
sea salt and freshly ground black pepper

1. Light the barbecue; it is ready when the flames have died down and the embers are glowing.

2. Bring a large saucepan of salted water to the boil. Add the sweetcorn cobs in their husks and cook for 4–5 minutes, then drain, allow to cool and pat dry with kitchen paper.

3. To make the spiced butter, place the soft butter in a bowl and add the honey, cayenne pepper and a good pinch of sea salt. Beat together to combine and set aside.

4. To make the herb dressing, place the mixed herbs, shallot, capers, garlic, lemon juice, olive oil and seasoning in a high-speed blender and blitz together until combined. (Alternatively chop the ingredients finely by hand and mix together in a bowl, seasoning well with salt and pepper.) Add a splash of water if needed, to loosen a little.

5. Once the corn cobs are cool enough to handle, peel back the husks to reveal the corn and remove the silky threads from inside. Tear off a strip of the green husk and use it to tie around the rest of the loose leaves to secure them. Place the corns on the hot grate and cook over direct heat for 8–10 minutes, turning frequently until charred. Move to indirect heat if they brown too quickly.

6. Remove the charred corn from the barbecue and arrange on a serving platter. While they are still hot, brush the spiced butter evenly over each corn cob, rotating so they are evenly coated and the butter oozes and melts.

7. Drizzle the herb dressing over the corn cobs and serve immediately.

MARCUS'S TIP

If you've made a batch of the spiced compound butter on page 33, that would also work beautifully on the corn instead of the one given here.

Lamb Ribs with Sweet Calvados Glaze

Ribs are one of the more affordable cuts of lamb and are perfect for slow cooking.
Adding a dry rub packs the meat full of flavour and the sticky glaze made with
calvados makes a real impact too. Calvados is an apple brandy made in Normandy
in the north of France; if you can't get it, a regular brandy will do the job.

SERVES: 4
PREP TIME: 20 MINUTES
COOKING TIME: 3 HOURS 25 MINUTES

2 tsp fennel seeds

2 tsp cumin seeds

1 tsp smoked paprika

1 tbsp chilli flakes

25g soft dark brown sugar

20g table salt

1 tbsp chopped fresh rosemary
leaves, plus whole sprigs for roasting

2 racks of lamb breast ribs (about
1.5kg each)

FOR THE GLAZE
200ml cider

100ml Calvados

7 tbsp runny honey

1. Toast the fennel and cumin seeds in a dry frying pan over medium heat until fragrant. Grind the toasted seeds in a pestle and mortar to a fine powder, then stir in the smoked paprika, chilli flakes, sugar, salt and chopped rosemary. Score the fat on the lamb ribs and cover well with this spice mixture, massaging it into the meat and fat. Set to one side.

2. For the glaze, put the cider and Calvados in a saucepan over medium heat and cook until the liquid is reduced by half. Stir in the honey and remove from the heat.

3. Light the barbecue; it is ready when the flames have died down and the embers are glowing.

4. Place the ribs onto the hot grate and cook for 15 minutes until charred, frequently brushing the ribs all over with the glaze. (To sear the ribs indoors, place the lamb ribs on a hot griddle pan and sear all over for a few minutes, or until golden.)

5. Meanwhile, preheat the oven to 160°C/140°C fan/gas 3. Place the ribs on a roasting tray, pour over any remaining glaze, add the sprigs of rosemary and cover tightly with foil. Cook in the hot oven for 3 hours until the meat is tender and begins to fall off the bone.

6. Remove the racks of lamb from the oven and carve them into individual ribs. Serve in a pile on a board.

Rib of Beef with Provençal Beans

This dish makes a really fabulous centrepiece for when you want to show off a bit:
a dry-rubbed rib of beef charred and cooked to perfection over the fire really can't
be beaten. The beans are inspired by the famous French vegetable dish, ratatouille,
which hails from Provence in the south of France. It's a tomato-based stew,
full of beautiful summer vegetables and I've also added some white beans
for extra flavour and texture.

SERVES: 4
PREP TIME: 30 MINUTES
COOKING TIME: 40 MINUTES, PLUS
15–20 MINUTES RESTING

1.5kg bone in
côte de boeuf (rib steaks)

1 tbsp mustard powder

1 tbsp olive oil

FOR THE SPICE RUB
1 tsp fennel seeds

1 tsp cumin seeds

½ tbsp dried oregano

1 tbsp smoked paprika

1 tbsp soft brown sugar

2 tbsp salt

FOR THE PROVENÇAL BEANS
4 tbsp olive oil

1 red onion, diced

1 red pepper, deseeded and diced

1 courgette, diced

1 aubergine, diced

3 garlic cloves, crushed

1 tbsp tomato purée

1 x 400g tin chopped tomatoes

300g jarred cannellini or haricot
beans, drained and rinsed

small handful of fresh basil or
parsley leaves, chopped

sea salt and freshly ground black
pepper

1. Rub the beef with the mustard and oil.

2. Toast the fennel and cumin seeds in a dry frying pan until fragrant,
   then grind in a pestle and mortar, with the oregano, smoked
   paprika, sugar and salt until well combined. Rub all over the meat
   and leave to marinate while you light the barbecue.

3. When the flames have died down and the embers are glowing,
   place the beef on the barbecue and cook for about 20 minutes on
   each side, moving all the time to get an even char all over. To test
   when the meat is cooked, insert a digital cooking thermometer into
   the thickest part of the meat: it should read 58–60°C. (To cook the
   beef indoors: preheat the oven to 220°C/200°C fan/gas 7, place
   the rib on a baking tray and roast for 20 minutes, then reduce the
   oven temperature to 160°C/140°C fan/gas 3 and roast for another
   20 minutes for medium or 15 minutes for rare.)

4. Rest the meat for 15–20 minutes before slicing.

5. While the beef is cooking make the beans. Heat half the oil in
   a large saucepan on the barbecue grate (or over medium heat
   indoors), then add the onion and pepper, season and gently fry
   for 4 minutes until soft. Tip into a bowl and return the pan to the
   heat. Add the remaining oil to the pan and fry the courgette and
   aubergine, covered with a lid, for 5–6 minutes, or until softened
   and just turning golden. Add the onions and peppers back to the
   pan along with the garlic and fry for 1–2 minutes, then add the
   tomato purée and fry for another minute. Add the chopped tinned
   tomatoes and 200ml of water, bring to a simmer, then cover and
   simmer for 15 minutes. Add the drained and rinsed beans, a little
   more water if it is looking at all dry, and simmer for another
   10 minutes. Check the seasoning and stir in the chopped herbs.

6. Slice the rested beef and serve with the beans on a large platter.

Charred Leeks with Roasted Red Pepper and Anchovy Dressing

Leeks are absolutely incredible when they're cooked over fire. The outer layer becomes charred and crisp while the inside of the leek steams and softens. And they can handle serious flavour too, so this dressing really packs a punch with raw garlic, anchovies and roasted red peppers. Topped with chopped almonds for some crunch, this is a really stunning side dish. If you're looking for a new addition to your barbecue repertoire, I urge you to give this one a go.

SERVES: 4 AS A SIDE DISH
PREP TIME: 15 MINUTES
COOKING TIME: 15 MINUTES

4 whole leeks, trimmed

olive oil

sea salt and freshly
ground black pepper

FOR THE DRESSING

1 x 50g tin anchovy fillets in oil

1 garlic clove, chopped

2 roasted red peppers from a jar,
deseeded

6 tbsp extra virgin olive oil

1 tbsp red wine vinegar

2 tsp honey

TO SERVE

25g whole almonds, toasted and
chopped

1 tbsp finely chopped fresh parsley
leaves

1. Light the barbecue; it is ready when the flames have died down and the embers are glowing.

2. Wash the leeks to remove any grit and pat dry with kitchen paper. Drizzle the leeks with olive oil and season well with salt and pepper. Rub evenly with the olive oil so they are nicely coated.

3. Add the whole leeks to the hot grate and cook for 12–15 minutes, turning frequently, until they are lovely and charred and softened, but still holding their shape.

4. To make the red pepper dressing, put all the ingredients into a high-speed blender or food processor with some salt and pepper and blend until smooth.

5. Cut the leeks in half lengthways and then arrange on a serving platter. Drizzle with the red pepper and anchovy dressing, serving any extra alongside. Scatter with the chopped almonds and parsley and serve.

MARCUS'S TIP

If you'd prefer to roast your own red peppers while you've got the barbecue lit, place them directly on the coals and cook until blackened all over. Then pop them in a bowl covered with clingfilm until the skins peel away easily. Remove all the skin and seeds and put the peppers into the blender along with the rest of the dressing ingredients.

Barbecued Piquant Red Pepper Spatchcock Chicken

Spatchcocking a chicken is where you remove the backbone and flatten it out. It's a great thing to do when you're cooking over fire because the whole chicken cooks evenly. It also gives you a much bigger surface area for the marinade to penetrate the meat, which results in extremely tasty chicken. I love to serve this with salad and aioli on the side.

SERVES: 4
PREP TIME: ABOUT 15 MINUTES, PLUS AT LEAST 2 HOURS MARINATING
COOKING TIME: ABOUT 1 HOUR, PLUS 10–15 MINUTES RESTING

1 large chicken (approx. 1.8kg)

FOR THE PIQUANT RED PEPPER MARINADE
2 banana shallots, roughly chopped
2 garlic cloves, chopped
½ tsp herbes de Provence (or dried mixed herbs)
1 tbsp red wine vinegar
1 roast pepper from jar, drained, deseeded and roughly chopped (approx. 70g)
1 red chilli, deseeded and chopped
1 tbsp soft dark brown sugar
3–4 tbsp olive oil
sea salt and freshly ground black pepper

TO SERVE
aioli (see page 149)
green salad

1. Firstly, make the marinade. Place the shallots, garlic, herbes de Provence, vinegar, pepper, chilli, sugar, olive oil and a good pinch of salt and pepper into a high-speed blender or food processor and blitz together until smooth and fully combined.

2. To spatchcock the chicken, use a sharp pair of scissors and cut down either side of the backbone, through the rib bones, to remove it. Turn the chicken over and flatten the breastbone with the palm of your hand so all the meat is a similar thickness. Score the chicken with a sharp knife, making deep slashes on the legs and breast meat. Place the chicken onto a shallow tray, pour over the marinade and use your hands to rub it into the chicken, covering it evenly all over. Allow to marinate for at least 2 hours (or ideally overnight).

3. Light the barbecue; it is ready when the flames have died down and the embers are glowing.

4. Cook the chicken skin side down on the hot grate over direct heat for 6–8 minutes until the chicken is golden brown and nicely charred. Turn over and cook for a further 5 minutes.

5. Move the chicken to the side part of the barbecue away from the direct heat, cover with the lid and cook at 180–200°C for about 50 minutes (depending on the size of your chicken). Keep an eye on the temperature (if your barbecue has a temperature gauge) so it stays consistent and cook until the chicken reaches 75°C on a digital cooking thermometer probe.

6. Once cooked, remove from the heat and transfer to a serving board. Cover with foil and allow to rest for 10–15 minutes.

7. Carve or shred the chicken and serve with aioli alongside and a green salad.

Brie-topped Burger with Mustard Mayonnaise and Grilled Potato Wedges

Who doesn't love a chargrilled cheeseburger cooked over fire on a summer's day? They're a real crowd-pleaser; to give mine a French twist I've topped them with slices of Brie, which melts beautifully on top of the beef, although Camembert or any French cheese would work as well. The potato wedges are a fabulous alternative to chips or French fries and are great for finishing off on the barbecue too – just make sure to get some grill marks on them for flavour and presentation. Photographed overleaf.

SERVES: 4
PREP TIME: 20–25 MINUTES,
PLUS 30 MINUTES CHILLING
COOKING TIME: ABOUT 35 MINUTES

FOR THE BURGERS
1 tbsp olive oil, plus extra for drizzling

1 red onion, finely chopped

500g good-quality beef mince

½ tsp garlic powder

few dashes of Tabasco

100g Brie, cut into slices

sea salt and freshly ground black pepper

FOR THE POTATO WEDGES
3 medium potatoes (approx. 750g) such as Desiree or Maris Piper

4 tbsp olive oil

good pinch of cayenne pepper

FOR THE MUSTARD MAYONNAISE
6 tbsp mayonnaise

2 heaped tsp Dijon mustard

1. To make the beef burgers, heat the olive oil in a medium frying pan and sauté the onion with a pinch of salt and pepper for 4–5 minutes to soften. Transfer to a large bowl and allow to cool. Add the beef mince, garlic powder, ½ teaspoon sea salt, ¼ teaspoon ground pepper and Tabasco and, using your hands, mix together to combine.

2. Shape the mixture into four burgers, pressing down gently to flatten a little and transfer to a large plate. Chill in the fridge for 30 minutes. Meanwhile, light the barbecue; it is ready when the flames have died down and the embers are glowing.

3. To prepare the wedges, cut each potato in half lengthways, then each half into four wedges. Bring a large saucepan of salted water to the boil and cook the potatoes for 8 minutes, or until tender. Drain and allow to steam dry.

4. Tip the potato wedges into a large bowl and drizzle with the olive oil, then season well with salt and sprinkle over the cayenne pepper. Toss to coat evenly.

5. For the mustard mayonnaise, mix the mayonnaise, mustard and some salt and pepper together in a bowl to combine. Set aside.

TO SERVE
4 brioche buns, split in half
4 little gem lettuce leaves
1 large beef tomato, sliced
gherkin or cucumber pickle slices

6. To cook the burgers, drizzle each burger with a little oil and place on the hot barbecue grate. Cook for about 5 minutes over direct heat until nicely browned, then carefully flip over and cook the other side for a further 4–5 minutes until cooked through. Move the burgers away from the direct heat, to the edge of the barbecue. Arrange the Brie slices on top of each burger, close the lid and allow to melt gently for a couple of minutes.

7. Lift the lid and arrange the potato wedges on the barbecue grate (keeping the burgers at the edge of the grate to keep warm) and cook over direct heat for 2–3 minutes on each side, or until golden and charred with grill marks. Remove and transfer to a serving plate and sprinkle with a little extra sea salt.

8. Toast the brioche buns cut side down on the barbecue for 1–2 minutes until lightly golden.

9. To assemble, spread a good dollop of mustard mayo onto each burger bun base. Top with a lettuce leaf and tomato slice and place the burger on top. Add a slice of gherkin then top with the bun lid and gently press together.

10. Serve the burger with the spiced wedges and any remaining mayonnaise.

MARCUS'S TIP

If you don't have a barbecue with a lid, place an upturned frying pan (as long as it doesn't have a plastic handle) over the burgers to melt the cheese.

Barbecued Fruits with Toasted Oat Crumble and Whipped Crème Fraîche

Barbecues aren't just for meat and veg – I love cooking desserts on them too. You can use any fruit you like, but stone fruits and melon work particularly well when cooked over fire. The fruit takes on a subtle smoky flavour and the natural sugars caramelise to create beautiful charring. I love serving the fruit with a toasted oaty, nutty crumble and crème fraîche on the side.

SERVES: 4–6
**PREP TIME: 10–15 MINUTES, PLUS
10–15 MINUTES RESTING**
COOKING TIME: 15–20 MINUTES

FOR THE BARBECUED FRUIT
2 peaches (or nectarines), halved and stones removed

2 apricots, halved and stones removed

2 plums, halved and stones removed

½ cantaloupe melon, cut into wedges

4 tbsp caster sugar

4 tbsp honey

1 vanilla pod, seeds scraped out

½ tsp ground cloves or mixed spice

FOR THE OAT CRUMBLE
50g plain flour

50g cold butter

50g jumbo porridge oats

30g Demerara sugar

finely grated nutmeg

50g pecans, chopped

pinch of sea salt

FOR THE WHIPPED CRÈME FRAÎCHE
200g crème fraîche

½ vanilla pod, seeds scraped out

finely grated nutmeg

1. Light the barbecue; it is ready when the flames have died down and the embers are glowing.

2. Place the prepared fruit into a large bowl. Sprinkle over the caster sugar, honey, vanilla seeds and pod and the ground cloves, then mix together and allow to sit for 10–15 minutes to release some of the juices.

3. Cook the fruit on the hot grate (reserving the syrupy juices left in the bowl) for 2–3 minutes on each side until charred and the fruit has softened but still holds it shape. Remove to a cooler part the barbecue to keep warm.

4. To make the crumble, put the flour and butter into a bowl and use your fingertips to rub together until the mixture resembles fine breadcrumbs. Stir in the oats, sugar, a little finely grated nutmeg, the pecans and a pinch of salt. Mix together to combine. Heat a large cast-iron skillet or non-stick frying pan on the barbecue until hot. Add the crumble topping and toast for 5–6 minutes, shaking the pan frequently, until the crumble is golden brown and evenly toasted.

5. Tip the reserved syrupy juices into a small saucepan along with 2–3 tablespoons of water and warm on the barbecue for a couple of minutes to thicken.

6. For the whipped crème fraîche, place the crème fraîche, vanilla seeds and a little grated nutmeg into a small bowl and using a handheld balloon whisk, whisk together until smooth and creamy.

7. To serve, arrange the fruit on a large serving platter and scatter the toasted crumble on top. Drizzle the syrup over the fruit and serve with the whipped crème fraîche alongside.

The French

Experience

My experience of eating in France has been nothing short of incredible; it's where I've had some of my most memorable meals. My stag do springs to mind as a great example. Gordon Ramsay was my best man and he took me to the south of France where we ate at Alain Ducasse's Le Louis XV in Monte Carlo. It was the absolute capital of gastronomy at the time – there was nothing else like it in Europe. The dining room was palatial and the thing that really sticks out in my memory is all the trolleys. There was a bread trolley, a champagne trolley, a cheese trolley, a liqueur trolley . . . you get the picture. (I definitely remember overindulging in the bread trolley!) I've been lucky enough to experience the cuisine of some of France's most iconic chefs: George Blanc's world-famous poulet à la crème, Joël Robuchon's pomme purée and Michel Bras' gargouillou, a pioneering vegetable-focused dish using twenty types of veg cooked in different ways. Not to mention when I worked in Paris for 10 months, where some of the best meals I ate were staff dinners at Guy Savoy. Guy always said that food for the staff was as important as food for the guests, so we'd have freshly baked bread and treats from the patisserie station. Which means I was also lucky enough to eat Guy's signature dessert: crème brûlée with apple crisps and jus de pomme.

This chapter encapsulates some of those once-in-a-lifetime meals, making them accessible for the home cook. I hope they create as many memories for you as they have for me.

Chicken Wings with Sticky Chilli and Apricot Glaze

Green Garden Soup with Garlic Snails

Artichokes Barigoule

Rosemary and Garlic Fougasse

Creamy Mussels with Pastis and Bayonne Ham

Mushroom and Jerusalem Artichoke Velouté
with Crispy Sage and Crushed Hazelnuts

French 'Pizzas': Tarte Flambée with Brie
and Onion, Pissaladière

Roast Chicken, Aioli and Garden Greens

Tartiflette

Millefeuille

Crème Brûlée with Dried Apple Slices

Plum and Armagnac Tart

Pistachio and Lemon Macarons

Pears Belle Hélène with Chocolate Orange Sauce

Chicken Wings with Sticky Chilli and Apricot Glaze

Anyone I know who's tried frogs legs in France – and I include myself on that list – says they taste like chicken, so this is my tribute to the classic French delicacy, using chicken wings. This is a great dish to have fun with the family. Giving the chicken wings both a rub and a glaze means they are super flavourful, and if you want to change up some of the spices to make this recipe your own then you absolutely can.

SERVES: 4
PREP TIME: 35 MINUTES, PLUS
30 MINUTES MARINATING
COOKING TIME: 30–40 MINUTES

1kg chicken wings, tips removed

FOR THE RUB
30g soft dark brown sugar
2 tsp garlic powder
2 tsp smoked paprika
½ tsp cayenne pepper
1 tsp sea salt

FOR THE GLAZE
75g apricot jam
2 tbsp sriracha sauce / hot chilli sauce
1 tbsp dark brown soft sugar
2 tsp white wine vinegar
sea salt and freshly ground black pepper

FOR THE SPICED YOGHURT DIP
175g natural yoghurt
2 heaped tsp sriracha
good pinch of smoked paprika
2 tbsp finely chopped fresh parsley and chives
2 spring onions, finely chopped

1. Preheat the oven to 220°C/200°C fan/gas 7.

2. To make the rub, mix everything in a large bowl to combine. Add the chicken wings and toss together to evenly coat in the rub. Set aside for 30 minutes to marinate.

3. Arrange the chicken wings in a single layer on a large baking tray. Roast for 25–30 minutes, turning once during cooking, until the wings are crisp, golden brown and cooked through.

4. For the glaze, mix all the ingredients together in a small saucepan with a good pinch of salt and pepper, whisking to combine. Place over low heat for 2–3 minutes until warmed through and the sugar has dissolved.

5. Remove the chicken wings from the oven and use a pastry brush to brush the sticky glaze over the wings to evenly coat. Return to the oven for a final 5–10 minutes, or until the wings are sticky and caramelised.

6. To make the dip, mix together the yoghurt, sriracha, paprika, herbs and spring onions in a bowl and season generously with salt and pepper to taste. Serve alongside the chicken wings.

Green Garden Soup with Garlic Snails

I think soups can be massively underrated, but my wife Jane and I love them. When I worked in Paris, Jane moved there with me and we lived in a tiny apartment together. We didn't get to eat out too often but when we did, this is just the sort of dish we'd try. The snails are totally optional, but I encourage you to give them a go; they are absolutely delicious smothered in herb and garlic butter.

SERVES: 4 (MAKES 1.3 LITRES)
PREP TIME: 20 MINUTES
COOKING TIME: ABOUT 20 MINUTES

2 tbsp olive oil, plus extra for drizzling

1 onion, finely chopped

2 courgettes, chopped

2 garlic cloves, chopped

200g fresh or frozen peas

800ml good-quality chicken or vegetable stock

125g fresh watercress

½ bunch of fresh chives (10g)

½ bunch of fresh dill (10g)

sea salt and freshly ground black pepper

edible flowers, pea shoots and fresh soft garden herbs, to finish (optional)

FOR THE GARLIC SNAILS
12 snail shells

12 tinned or jarred snails, drained

75g herbed garlic butter
(see page 33)

1. Heat the olive oil in a saucepan over medium heat, add the onion, courgettes and garlic, season well and fry for 10 minutes, or until softened. Add the peas and stock and bring to the boil. Add the watercress, remove from the heat and stir until it is wilted. Add the chives and dill and then blend with a stick blender until smooth.

2. Preheat the oven to 180C°/160°C fan/gas 4.

3. Lay the snail shells on a baking tray, place a snail into each one and then top with a little of the herbed garlic butter. Bake for 10–12 minutes, or until the butter is bubbling hot.

4. Divide the soup among four bowls and finish with a drizzle of olive oil, some cracked black pepper, edible flowers, pea shoots and any soft herbs from the garden (if using). Top with 3 hot snails per bowl and serve.

MARCUS'S TIP

If snails aren't your cup of tea, swap them out for some crispy croutons. Just fry cubes of bread in oil until golden brown, sprinkle them over the soup and drizzle some of the melted herby garlic butter over the top.

Artichokes Barigoule

This is a dish I remember learning at college but never really enjoying. It wasn't until I had the privilege of cooking it recently with a fabulous chef at a family-run restaurant in Provence that I discovered just how delicious it could be. In fact it was the best thing I ate on that entire trip. It's fresh, clean and simple, but the depth of flavour gained from cooking the artichokes in wine and stock with carrots, bacon and – the surprise ingredient, lettuce – is remarkable. Photographed overleaf.

SERVES: 4
PREP TIME: 40–45 MINUTES
COOKING TIME: 30–40 MINUTES

1 lemon

8–12 baby globe artichokes (2 or 3 per person, depending on size)

2 tbsp olive oil

100g smoked bacon lardons, diced

1 large onion, finely diced

2 large carrots, peeled and finely diced

12 small pearl onions or small shallots, peeled

2 garlic cloves, crushed

bunch of fresh flat-leaf parsley, thyme sprigs and 2 bay leaves, tied together with string

300ml white wine

400ml good-quality chicken stock

¼ round lettuce, finely shredded

1 tbsp butter

sea salt and freshly ground black pepper

1. Fill a large bowl with cold water and squeeze in the juice of half the lemon.

2. Next prepare the artichokes. Peel off the dark green outer leaves of the artichokes and peel the stem with a small sharp knife or peeler to remove the fibrous outer layer, then cut off the spiky tops of the leaves on each artichoke. Scoop out and discard the hairy chokes using a small spoon, leaving the heart below, and immediately place in the lemon water to stop them from browning.

3. Heat the olive oil in a large ovenproof casserole dish, add the bacon lardons, onion and carrots to the casserole dish, season well and fry for 6–8 minutes, or until softened and just turning golden. Add the prepared artichokes and pearl onions or shallots and brown on all sides for a few more minutes. Add the garlic and fry for another minute or two.

4. Add the herbs tied with string and the white wine, then increase the heat and cook over medium-high heat for 3–4 minutes, or until the liquid has reduced by half and the alcohol has evaporated.

Continued Overleaf...

5. Pour over the chicken stock and bring to the boil. Cover with a lid, reduce the heat and simmer for 15–20 minutes, or until the artichokes are tender when poked with a knife. The time this takes will depend on the size of the artichokes – the larger they are the longer they will take to cook. Add the shredded lettuce and allow to wilt for 30 seconds, then remove the pan from the heat. Remove and discard the herbs.

6. Place the artichokes on a serving dish. Leave any cooking liquid in the pan, place this mixture over a medium heat, add the butter and a squeeze of lemon juice and simmer until the sauce has thickened slightly. Pour this sauce over the top of the artichokes and serve warm.

MARCUS'S TIP

This is a fantastic dish to make ahead, as the flavours develop over time. It will keep in the fridge for a day or two. I would recommend holding back the lettuce and adding it when you reheat the dish just before serving.

Rosemary and Garlic Fougasse

Bread is certainly something that France is famous for all over the world; this is one of the loaves that would definitely have appeared on the bread trolley that I mentioned in the introduction to this chapter of the book. It's similar in style to an Italian focaccia, flavoured with olive oil, sea salt and fresh rosemary, but its distinctive shape sets it apart and makes it look not only decorative, but impressive too. Photographed overleaf.

MAKES: 4
PREP TIME: 30 MINUTES,
PLUS ABOUT 1½ HOURS PROVING
COOKING TIME: 15 MINUTES

500g strong white bread flour, plus extra for dusting

1 x 7g sachet instant yeast

1 tsp sea salt, plus extra for sprinkling

4 sprigs of fresh rosemary, leaves picked and chopped

4–6 garlic cloves, finely chopped

2 tbsp olive oil, plus extra for greasing

300ml warm water

FOR THE TOPPING
drizzle of olive oil

2 sprigs of fresh rosemary

1 tsp sea salt

1. Put the flour, yeast, sea salt, rosemary and garlic into a stand mixer fitted with the dough hook. With the motor running, gradually pour in the olive oil and warm water and knead on a medium-high setting for about 10 minutes, or until the dough is smooth, elastic and soft. Add more flour if the dough is too sticky. (Alternatively, if making by hand, place the flour, yeast, salt, rosemary and garlic into a large bowl. Add the oil and pour in the warm water, mixing by hand until combined. Turn out onto a heavily floured work surface and knead for around 10 minutes.)

2. Place the dough into a large bowl lightly greased with a little oil and cover with a clean, damp tea towel. Leave to prove for 40 minutes–1 hour until it has doubled in size and springs back when touched.

3. Turn the dough out onto a floured work surface, knock back and lightly knead for a couple of minutes. Cut the dough into four equal pieces. Roll or press each piece of dough into a rough rectangular/oval shape, measuring 18 × 25cm and 5mm thick. Transfer the breads to four large baking sheets, dusted with flour (or lined with baking parchment). Using a sharp serrated knife, make a large cut

down the centre of each rectangle (the long side) leaving around 1–2cm gap from each end. Make three or four more cuts diagonally on either side, carefully stretching each hole with floured hands until the bread resembles a leaf shape (you need to ensure the holes are big enough so they don't close up when baking). Lightly drizzle each bread with olive oil then carefully press in the extra rosemary sprigs at intervals to decorate, then sprinkle with sea salt. Cover again with a damp tea towel and leave to prove for 30 minutes.

4. Preheat the oven to 240°C/220°C fan/gas 8.

5. Once the breads have proved for the second time, sprinkle with sea salt and bake in the hot oven for 15 minutes until golden brown and crisp.

MARCUS'S TIP

I've suggested this recipe makes four small loaves, but you could instead divide the dough in half to make two larger ones. You can also let your imagination run wild with the shape and design of the loaves. Sometimes I like to make cuts around the edges to create points that go nice and crispy when they're baked.

Creamy Mussels with Pastis and Bayonne Ham

We all know the classic French mussel recipe moules marinière, but I love this version. It's much more soupy, meaning lots of opportunity for bread dunking. It has an incredibly flavourful punch of aniseed from the pastis and a rich, salty taste of ham, which is both cooked with the mussels and sprinkled on top. I've used Bayonne ham, but you can really use any cured ham that you like.

SERVES: 4
PREP TIME: 10 MINUTES
COOKING TIME: ABOUT 35 MINUTES

2kg fresh mussels

2 tbsp olive oil

50g unsalted butter

4 shallots, finely chopped

4 garlic cloves, crushed

8 slices of Bayonne ham, shredded

100ml pastis

150ml dry white wine

150ml fish stock

150ml double cream

handful of fresh chopped mixed soft herbs, to include parsley, tarragon and chives

sea salt and freshly ground black pepper

TO SERVE

1 lemon, cut into wedges

crusty bread

1. Firstly prepare the mussels. Pull off the beards at the hinged end of the shell and wash the mussels in a colander under cold running water to remove grit. Scrub off any large barnacles and discard broken or open mussels, or any that do not close when you tap them against a work surface.

2. Heat the oil in a deep saucepan (with a lid) and melt the butter and olive oil over medium heat. Add the shallots and garlic and a little seasoning and sauté for 4–5 minutes, stirring frequently until the shallots are softened but not browned. Add half the Bayonne ham and cook for a further 2–3 minutes.

3. Pour in the pastis and white wine, bring to the boil and then simmer for 10 minutes until reduced. Add the fish stock. Simmer for a further 5 minutes. Add the cleaned mussels, cover with a lid, turn the heat up and cook over high heat for 4–5 minutes until all the mussel shells have opened.

4. Strain the liquor through a colander into a medium saucepan. Keep the mussels hot by returning to the large cooking pan and covering with a lid. Discard any unopened mussels, making sure you reserve all the shallot and ham pieces.

5. Bring the liquor back to the boil over medium heat, whisk in the cream and cook for a few minutes until thickened. Stir in the chopped herbs and check the seasoning; go lightly with any salt as the ham will be salty.

6. Divide the mussels, ham and shallots among four serving bowls and generously spoon the sauce over each. Scatter with the remaining shredded ham. Serve with the lemon wedges and crusty bread alongside.

Mushroom and Jerusalem Artichoke Velouté with Crispy Sage and Crushed Hazelnuts

Technically a velouté has a roux base made with flour, which gives it body and richness; I've had a version of this in Paris and it was exactly that. I wanted to recreate the recipe I'd eaten, but with a lighter feel so I've left the roux out, making it more of a smooth, blended soup. The crispy sage and toasted hazelnut toppings are like little flavour bombs that give texture as well as great taste.

SERVES: 4
PREP TIME: 15 MINUTES
COOKING TIME: ABOUT 40 MINUTES

1 tbsp olive oil

30g unsalted butter

1 onion, sliced

2 garlic cloves, crushed

2 sprigs of fresh tarragon

2 sprigs of fresh thyme

400g Jerusalem artichokes, peeled and sliced

200g chestnut mushrooms, sliced

200g button mushrooms, sliced

splash of white wine

1 litre good-quality chicken or vegetable stock, plus a little extra if needed

75ml double cream

sea salt and freshly ground black pepper

TO SERVE

1 tbsp extra virgin olive oil

handful of fresh sage leaves

extra virgin olive oil

50g hazelnuts, toasted and lightly crushed

1. Heat the oil and butter in a large, wide saucepan over medium heat. Once hot, add the onion, garlic, tarragon and thyme sprigs and a good pinch of salt and pepper and cook for 10–12 minutes until softened and the onion is caramelised.

2. Increase the heat and add the Jerusalem artichokes and chestnut and button mushrooms. Cook for 10 minutes until the liquid released from the mushrooms has evaporated. Pour in the white wine and reduce for a couple of minutes before adding the stock. Reduce the heat and simmer gently for 12–15 minutes.

3. Remove the thyme and tarragon sprigs from the pan and transfer the velouté to a blender or food processor. Blitz until smooth, then pass through a sieve into a clean saucepan and stir in the cream. Check the seasoning and warm through gently, adding a splash of extra stock if needed to slightly loosen.

4. For the crispy sage, heat the olive oil in a frying pan over medium-high heat. Once hot add the sage leaves and cook for 30 seconds to 1 minute on each side until crisp. Immediately transfer to a plate lined with kitchen paper.

5. To serve, ladle the velouté into soup bowls and arrange the crispy sage leaves on top. Drizzle with a little extra virgin olive oil and sprinkle over the crushed hazelnuts.

French 'Pizzas'

These recipes are often described as France's answer to pizza, although I have to say, in my mind, they're unmistakably French. Both have dough bases, topped with caramelised onions, but that's where the similarities end. Tarte Flambée comes from the Alsace region and has a layer of melted cheese on top, while Pissaladière (photographed overleaf), hails from Nice in the south of France and is classically adorned with salty anchovies and black olives. Both are completely moreish.

Tarte Flambée with Brie and Onion

SERVES: 4 AS A LIGHT LUNCH
PREP TIME: 30 MINUTES,
PLUS 30 MINUTES CHILLING
COOKING TIME: ABOUT 50 MINUTES

FOR THE STICKY ONIONS
1 tbsp olive oil

2 red onions (approx. 200g), thinly sliced

½ tsp salt

75ml ruby port

125ml good-quality beef stock

1 tbsp red wine vinegar

1 tbsp Demerara sugar

freshly ground black pepper

FOR THE DOUGH
175g plain flour, plus extra for dusting

¼ tsp table salt

½ tsp dried thyme

½ tsp onion powder

3 tbsp olive oil

FOR THE TOPPING
175g Brie, thickly sliced

1 tbsp finely chopped fresh thyme leaves

olive oil

1. To make the sticky onions, heat the olive oil in a sauté pan, add the sliced onions, salt and a generous pinch of pepper and fry over medium heat for 10–15 minutes, or until softened and golden. Add the ruby port and reduce for 5–6 minutes, or until all the alcohol has evaporated. Add the stock and cook for 8 minutes, or until it has reduced and thickened and almost all the liquid has evaporated. Next add the red wine vinegar and sugar and cook over low heat for 3–4 minutes to a jam-like consistency. Remove from the heat and leave to cool.

2. To make the dough, combine the flour, salt, thyme and onion powder in a bowl, then add 100ml of cold water and the olive oil and bring everything together with a blunt knife or spoon to form a dough. Transfer to a floured work surface and knead for 3–5 minutes until you have a smooth dough. Alternatively, make the dough in a stand mixer fitted with the dough hook. Shape the dough into a ball, then flatten it slightly to form a disc and wrap in clingfilm. Rest in the fridge for 30 minutes.

3. Preheat the oven to 220°C/200°C fan/gas 7.

4. Dust a work surface lightly with flour and roll out the pastry into a 30 × 20cm rectangle. Transfer to a floured baking sheet.

5. To assemble the tarte, spread the cooled onions over the dough, leaving a 1cm border clear around the edge. Arrange slices of Brie over the onions, then sprinkle with the fresh thyme and drizzle with olive oil. Bake in the oven for 18–20 minutes until the base is crisp and the cheese has started to caramelise. Remove from the oven and serve immediately.

Pissaladière

SERVES: 4
PREP TIME: 25–30 MINUTES,
PLUS 1 HOUR PROVING
COOKING TIME: ABOUT 1 HOUR
10 MINUTES

FOR THE DOUGH

250g strong white bread flour, plus extra for dusting

3.5g instant yeast (½ x 7g sachet)

½ tsp sea salt, plus extra for sprinkling

1 tbsp olive oil, plus extra for greasing

150ml warm water

FOR THE CARAMELISED ONIONS

2 tbsp olive oil, plus extra for drizzling

knob of butter

4 large onions (approx. 600g), sliced

4 garlic cloves, thinly sliced

4 sprigs of fresh thyme, leaves chopped, plus a few whole leaves for scattering

2 tsp soft dark brown sugar

1 tbsp red wine vinegar

1. Put the flour, yeast and sea salt into a stand mixer fitted with the dough hook. With the motor running, gradually pour in the olive oil and warm water and knead on medium-high setting for about 10 minutes until the dough is smooth, elastic and soft. (Alternatively, if making by hand, add the flour, yeast and salt to a large bowl. Add the oil and pour in the warm water, mixing by hand until combined. Turn out onto a heavily floured work surface and knead for around 10 minutes.)

2. Place the dough into a large bowl lightly greased with a little oil and cover with a clean, damp tea towel. Leave to prove for 40 minutes– 1 hour until it has doubled in size and springs back when touched.

3. While the dough is proving make the caramelised onions for the topping. Heat the olive oil and butter in a large, non-stick sauté or frying pan. Add the onions, garlic and thyme leaves along with a pinch of seasoning and cook over medium-low heat for 20–25 minutes, stirring frequently, until they are softened and starting to take on some colour.

4. Stir in the sugar and vinegar, increase the heat a little and cook for a further 15–20 minutes until the onions are richly caramelised, sticky and dark. Set aside and allow to cool.

5. Preheat the oven to 220°C/200°C fan/gas 7.

Continued Overleaf …

FOR THE TOPPING

2 tbsp Dijon mustard

3 x 50g tins of anchovies in oil, drained

100g black olives, pitted

sea salt and freshly ground black pepper

6. Once the dough has proved, turn out onto a floured work surface, knock back and lightly knead for a couple of minutes. Roll out into a rectangular shape about 35 × 25cm and then press into an oiled baking tray that is the same size (there is no need to allow it to prove again).

7. Spread the Dijon mustard across the base of the dough, leaving a 1–2cm border around the edge. Once the onions are cool, spread them on top. Arrange the anchovies on top of the onions, in a criss-cross fashion, or more relaxed if you prefer. Scatter the black olives on top, either at the crossing points or in a more rustic style, making sure the onions are evenly covered. Drizzle with a little oil.

8. Bake in the oven for 20–25 minutes until the dough is risen and golden brown. Remove from the oven and scatter with thyme leaves before cutting into pieces.

Roast Chicken, Aioli and Garden Greens

A love of a good roast chicken dinner is something we have in common with the French; in fact, the only real difference with theirs is that they don't tend to have gravy. But fear not because there is a sauce from Provence that is almost as perfect with roast chicken and that's aioli, a garlicky mayonnaise. It happens to be amazing with roast potatoes too! Next time you're planning a Sunday roast, give this one a go.

SERVES: 4
PREP TIME: 30 MINUTES
COOKING TIME: ABOUT 2 HOURS

1 tsp fennel seeds

1 tsp dried chilli flakes

1 tsp dried oregano

1 tsp smoked paprika

½ tsp garlic powder

2 tsp sea salt

1 tbsp soft light brown sugar

grated zest of 1 lime

1 chicken (about 1.5kg)

1 lemon, sliced

bunch of fresh garden herbs, finely chopped

olive oil, for drizzling

250ml white wine

1. Preheat the oven to 200°C/180°C fan/gas 6.

2. To make the rub for the chicken, grind together the fennel seeds, chilli flakes, oregano, paprika, garlic powder and salt to a fine powder in a pestle and mortar. Stir in the sugar and lime zest.

3. Place the chicken in a roasting tin, stuff the cavity with the lemon slices and herbs and drizzle the skin with olive oil. Rub the spice mix all over the chicken until it is fully coated, then pour a splash of white wine into the base of the roasting tray. Cook for 1 hour and 15–20 minutes, basting occasionally with the juices in the base of the tray. The chicken is cooked through when the juices run clear with no trace of pink when the thickest part of the leg (between the drumstick and the thigh) is pierced with a skewer.

4. Roast the garlic for the charred garden greens. Place the garlic bulb on a piece of foil, drizzle with a little olive oil and add a good pinch of salt and pepper. Wrap and place in the oven for 30 minutes, or until the garlic is soft, sticky and golden.

5. Meanwhile, make the aioli: put the egg yolks, crushed garlic, lemon juice, mustard and a pinch of salt in a blender. With the blender on the slowest setting, slowly add the oil in a thin stream. If it begins to thicken too much, add a little more lemon juice. Repeat this process until all the oil is blended in and the mixture has emulsified. Add a splash of water if the aioli is too thick. Finely chop the herbs and add to the aioli, then season to taste.

6. When the chicken is cooked through, let it rest for 10 minutes before portioning.

Continued Overleaf …

FOR THE CHARRED GARDEN GREENS

1 whole garlic bulb

2 tbsp olive oil, plus extra for drizzling over the garlic

800g mixed seasonal greens (such as cavolo nero and purple sprouting broccoli)

juice of 1 lemon

handful of fresh garden herbs such as basil, chives and parsley

sea salt and freshly ground black pepper

FOR THE AIOLI

2 egg yolks

2 garlic cloves, crushed

juice of ½ lemon

1 tbsp Dijon mustard

300ml mix of vegetable oil and olive oil

small handful of fresh garden herbs such as basil, parsley, tarragon and chives

7. To make the charred garden greens, prepare and wash your chosen greens: remove any tough stems from the cavolo nero and roughly tear or chop the leaves. Steam the broccoli for 2 minutes and then griddle on a hot griddle pan drizzled with half the olive oil and some salt and pepper until lightly charred all over. Tip onto a serving dish and repeat with the cavolo nero. Squeeze the roasted garlic cloves out of their skins and add to the greens with the lemon juice and herbs and toss together.

8. Serve the chicken with the greens and aioli alongside.

MARCUS'S TIP

To carve a roast chicken, first remove the wings by stretching them away from the body of the chicken, cut through the skin at the knuckle, then cut through the joint. You're not cutting through bone, rather the space between the bones at the joint. This goes for the legs, too. Pull the leg away from the body and cut the skin as close to the leg as possible, leaving as much of the skin attached to the breast as you can. Expose the joint and cut through. Now separate the drumstick from the thigh; place the leg skin-side down on the board, feel for the joint between the drumstick and thigh and cut through. Next, remove the breasts by running your knife down one side of the breastbone, keeping it as close to the carcass as you can, and cut until the breast comes away. Repeat on the other side. You can then carve the breast meat into slices. It's much easier to do this once the breast has been removed. Pick off any remaining bits of meat from the carcass and save the carcass itself for making stock, soup or gravy; it will keep in the freezer.

Tartiflette

This is the ultimate comfort food: layers of potato, bacon, onion and Reblochon cheese baked together until bubbly and golden brown. It comes from the Aosta Valley in the French Alps and is very popular, especially in the wintertime. My family and I have eaten many a tartiflette on skiing holidays as it's the perfect dish to warm you up after a day on the slopes. Reblochon cheese is key to this dish and it is available in lots of supermarkets. However if you can't find it, try a Camembert instead, it will still be delicious if not traditional.

SERVES: 6
PREP TIME: 20 MINUTES
COOKING TIME: ABOUT 1 HOUR

1kg Charlotte potatoes, peeled and halved if large

2 tbsp olive oil

250g smoked bacon lardons

2 onions, thinly sliced

2 garlic cloves, crushed

100ml white wine

200ml double cream

2 sprigs of fresh thyme, leaves picked

450g Reblochon cheese

sea salt and freshly ground black pepper

green salad with a sharp mustard dressing, to serve

1. Add the potatoes to a large saucepan of boiling salted water and cook for 10–15 minutes, or until just tender. Drain and allow to cool slightly and then cut the potatoes into thin slices. Set aside.

2. While the potatoes are cooking, add the olive oil to a sauté pan, add the bacon lardons, onions and a little seasoning, and cook over medium heat for 15 minutes, or until golden. Add the garlic and fry for another minute or two. Pour the white wine into the pan to deglaze and cook over medium-high heat for 2–3 minutes, or until the liquid has almost all gone.

3. Preheat the oven to 180°C/160°C fan/gas 4.

4. Layer the sliced potatoes and bacon/onion mixture in alternating layers into an ovenproof dish that is approx. 26 × 20cm. Pour over the cream, scatter over the thyme leaves and add a grind of pepper, then slice the Reblochon and place over the top in an even layer.

5. Bake in the oven for 20–25 minutes, or until golden and bubbling. Serve hot with a dressed green salad.

Millefeuille

Millefeuilles are hands down my favourite pastry. I had a particular weakness for them when I lived in Paris and would stop at a patisserie to buy one as often as I could afford to. Millefeuille literally means 'a thousand leaves', referring to the layers and layers of flaky puff pastry, which I'm sure in the Parisian patisseries was all made from scratch. However, these days in my kitchen, a good old shop-bought puff pastry does the job, meaning I can whip up a batch and indulge my habit in no time at all. Any leftover custard will keep in the fridge for a few days. Photographed overleaf.

MAKES: 4
PREP TIME: 25 MINUTES, PLUS COOLING AND CHILLING
COOKING TIME: ABOUT 20 MINUTES

1 x 320g sheet of ready-rolled all-butter puff pastry

flour, for dusting

250g raspberries or blackberries (or a mix)

FOR THE PASTRY CREAM
300ml milk

50ml double cream

seeds from 1 vanilla pod

4 egg yolks

60g caster sugar

30g cornflour

FOR THE ICING
100g icing sugar, sifted

1 tbsp soft butter

juice of ½ lemon

1 tbsp boiling water

1. Line a baking sheet with baking parchment.

2. Unroll the puff pastry sheet on a floured work surface and then cut it into twelve 6 × 9cm rectangles. Arrange them on the lined baking sheet, prick them all over with the prongs of a fork, then place back in the fridge for 20 minutes.

3. Preheat the oven to 200°C/180°C fan/gas 6.

4. Cover the chilled pastry rectangles with another sheet of baking parchment and another baking sheet. Bake for 18–20 minutes until golden. Remove from the oven, take off the top baking sheet and sheet of parchment and leave to cool completely on a wire rack.

5. To make the pastry cream, put the milk, cream and vanilla seeds in a medium saucepan and bring just to the boil, stirring frequently. Put the egg yolks, sugar and cornflour into a heatproof bowl and whisk until smooth. Slowly pour in a third of the hot milk, whisking continuously. Reduce the heat to medium-low and then add the egg mix to the milk mix in the pan. Cook over very low heat, stirring constantly, until it comes to a low simmer, then simmer for 2 minutes until thickened. Take care not to boil the custard as the egg yolks will scramble. If the hot custard is lumpy, pass it through a fine sieve into a container. Cover the surface of the custard with clingfilm (to prevent a skin forming) and chill.

6. To make the icing, whisk the icing sugar in a bowl with the butter, lemon juice and the boiling water until smooth. Place four of the pastry rectangles on a piece of baking parchment and ice the tops.

7. Pipe all of the custard onto eight of the rectangles, dotting raspberries and blackberries between the custard. Assemble each millefeuille with two layers of custard-topped pastry, finish with the iced pastry rectangles and gently press. Chill for 20 minutes before serving.

MARCUS'S TIP

Chilling the pastry before baking it ensures the butter doesn't melt too quickly in the oven and spill out of the pastry, which would prevent the all-important layers from forming, so don't be tempted to skip this stage.

Crème Brûlée with Dried Apple Slices

When I worked at three-Michelin-starred restaurant Guy Savoy in Paris, my favourite dessert on the menu was crème brûlée with apple crisps and jus de pomme. I've always remembered how good the combination was: rich and creamy set custard, crispy sugar topping and delicate apple flavour. I've used that dish as inspiration for this recipe, simply serving apple crisps to dunk into the crème brûlée for something a little bit different.

SERVES: 4
PREP TIME: 30 MINUTES
COOKING TIME: ABOUT 2 HOURS
35 MINUTES, PLUS 3–4 HOURS
COOLING

FOR THE CRÈME BRÛLÉE
400ml double cream

1 vanilla pod, split lengthways and seeds scraped out

5 egg yolks

40g caster sugar

4 heaped tsp Demerara sugar, for sprinkling

FOR THE DRIED APPLE SLICES
1 apple such as Pink Lady, skin on and kept whole

caster sugar, for sprinkling

freshly grated nutmeg

1. First make the dried apple slices. Preheat the oven to 100°C/80°C fan/gas ¼.

2. Using an apple corer, remove the core and slice the apple into thin rings, about 2–3mm thick. Arrange on a large baking tray lined with baking parchment. Sprinkle the apple slices with sugar and grate over a little nutmeg. Bake in the oven for 2 hours until dried and crisp, turning once during cooking. Turn off the oven and leave to dry in the oven for a few hours (or overnight).

3. Preheat the oven to 150°C/130°C fan/gas 2.

4. Put the cream and vanilla pod and seeds into a medium saucepan and heat until almost boiling. Immediately turn the heat off and allow to infuse for 10 minutes.

5. Whisk the egg yolks and caster sugar in a large bowl until pale and thickened. Gradually pour over the hot cream mixture, whisking continuously to combine, then strain into a jug. Place four ramekins (125ml) into a deep roasting tin and divide the custard evenly between each ramekin.

6. Pour hot water into the tin, so it reaches halfway up the sides of the ramekins. Bake in the oven for 30–35 minutes until just set. Remove from the oven, then remove the ramekins from the tin. Allow to cool for at least 3–4 hours, preferably overnight.

7. Once cool, sprinkle the top of each ramekin with a heaped teaspoon of Demerara sugar and caramelise using a blow torch or under a hot grill for 1–2 minutes, or until a dark golden brown colour. Allow to cool and serve when the top is hard and firm. Serve with the dried apple slices alongside.

Plum and Armagnac Tart

Armagnac is a type of brandy from the Gascony region in the southwest of France. It's made from a blend of different white grapes, setting it apart from cognac which only uses one grape variety. It's aged in oak barrels for years, which gives it a complex taste. I've had it often in France as a digestif but have to say I much prefer cooking with it. Prunes in Armagnac is a classic combination in France, but it pairs perfectly with plums too. You will need a fluted, loose-bottomed tart tin, 23cm in diameter and 3cm deep. Photographed overleaf.

SERVES: 8–10
PREP TIME: 40 MINUTES, PLUS 50 MINUTES CHILLING
COOKING TIME: ABOUT 1 HOUR 20 MINUTES, PLUS 15 MINUTES COOLING

FOR THE PLUMS
5 fresh plums, halved and stones removed
4 tbsp Armagnac
2–3 tbsp caster sugar
peeled zest of ½ orange
1 cinnamon stick

FOR THE PASTRY
175g plain flour, plus extra for dusting
pinch of fine sea salt
115g cold butter, diced
50g icing sugar
1 egg yolk
1–2 tbsp cold water

1. Preheat the oven to 180°C/160°C fan/gas 4.

2. Arrange the plums cut side up in a roasting tray so that they fit snugly in. Pour over the Armagnac, then scatter over the sugar, strips of orange zest and cinnamon stick. Cover with foil and bake for 20 minutes, or until tender but holding shape.

3. For the pastry, rub together the flour, salt and butter until you have a breadcrumb-like texture (or blitz in a food processor). Stir in the icing sugar and gradually add the egg yolk and cold water to form a soft, pliable dough. Shape into a disc, wrap in clingfilm and chill for 30 minutes.

4. Place the rested pastry dough onto a lightly floured work surface and roll it out wide enough to cover the tart tin with 1–2cm hanging over the edge. Sprinkle your rolling pin with a little more flour, then carefully lift the pastry onto the pin and into the tart tin. Dip your fingers in a little flour so they don't stick to the pastry, then carefully press the pastry into the base and the grooves in the sides of the tin – it will hang over the edges a little. Be careful not to stretch the pastry as this will cause tears or make it shrink in the oven.

5. Increase the oven temperature to 220°C/200°C fan/gas 7.

6. Prick the pastry base a few times with a fork so it doesn't puff up during baking. Cut a circle of baking parchment a little larger than the tin so it overhangs a little, place on top of the pastry and fill this with ceramic baking beans or uncooked rice/dried beans. Place in the fridge and chill for 20 minutes, or until the pastry is firm to touch.

Continued Overleaf...

FOR THE FRANGIPANE

150g caster sugar

150g soft butter

3 eggs

pinch of sea salt

185g ground almonds

TO SERVE

custard (optional)

7. Place the tin onto a baking sheet and 'blind bake' for 15 minutes until it starts to turn golden and become firm. Remove the baking parchment and baking beans and bake for another 5 minutes, or until the pastry is evenly golden and crisp. Remove from the oven and allow to cool slightly. When cool enough to handle, trim away the excess pastry from the edges of the tart case with a small sharp knife.

8. Reduce the oven temperature to 180°C/160°C fan/gas 4.

9. To make the frangipane, beat together the sugar and butter until light and creamy. Add the eggs one at a time, beating well after each addition. Finally mix in the pinch of salt and the ground almonds.

10. Blitz three of the cooked plum halves in a blender or food processor until you have a smooth purée, then spread this over the base of the pastry case, followed by the frangipane. Arrange the remaining plum halves on top, cut side up. Bake for 40–45 minutes until it is deep golden and the frangipane has just set in the centre. Cool for at least 15 minutes before brushing the plums with the remaining plum baking juices and serving with custard, if you like.

MARCUS'S TIP

Fresh plums can vary in sweetness depending on the season and how ripe they are, so if yours are very tart, use a little more caster sugar to bake the plums. If you can't find fresh plums for this recipe, tinned will also work nicely.

Pistachio and Lemon Macarons

Macarons are made from a meringue base, typically mixed with ground almonds.
But I'm changing up the key flavour by using pistachios instead. Blitzing them in a
food processor with icing sugar creates a fine powder, similar in texture to ground
almonds. It works so well and gives amazing flavour. Pistachios aren't always as
green as you might imagine so if you'd like your finished macarons to be more
intensely green, add some gel food colouring to the mix (but don't be tempted to
use liquid food colouring as this will affect the rise of the macarons).
Photographed overleaf.

MAKES: 16
PREP TIME: 35 MINUTES, PLUS
40–60 MINUTES RESTING
COOKING TIME: ABOUT 15 MINUTES,
PLUS COOLING

FOR THE MACARONS
90g green shelled pistachios

125g icing sugar

2 egg whites, at room temperature

pinch of fine salt

65g caster sugar

a few drops green gel food colouring
(optional)

FOR THE LEMON CURD FILLING
80ml fresh lemon juice

50g caster sugar

1 egg, plus 2 egg yolks (from the
macaron mix)

80g soft butter, cubed

1. Pulse the pistachios in a blender or food processor until they are finely chopped. Add the icing sugar and blend again until they are well combined. Pass this mixture through a sieve to ensure you have a very fine nutty powder, then blend again any bits that are not fine enough to pass through the sieve. Set aside.

2. Place the egg whites into a very clean glass bowl, add a pinch of salt and then whisk with an electric whisk until they form soft peaks. Add the caster sugar a little at a time, whisking well between each addition. Repeat until all the sugar has been incorporated and the mix is stiff and glossy. You should be able to turn the bowl upside down without the meringue mix falling out.

3. Add the sifted pistachio and icing sugar mix and carefully fold into the beaten egg whites. Add a little green gel food colouring if you want a more vibrant green colour.

4. Line two large baking sheets with silicone baking mats or baking parchment and draw 16 evenly spaced 4.5cm circles on each one (or use silicone macaron mats). Try to keep the circles in neat lines, with about 3–4cm between each one.

5. Spoon the macaron batter into a piping bag fitted with a medium round 1cm piping tip. Holding the piping bag at a 90-degree angle over the baking sheet, pipe 32 evenly sized macarons onto the prepared baking sheets, using the circles as a guide. Gently press down any peaks on the top of each macaron with a damp finger. Bang the baking sheets a couple times on the work surface to pop any air bubbles, then use a toothpick to pop any bubbles that remain.

6. Let the piped macarons sit at room temperature until they are dry and no longer tacky to touch on top. This usually takes about 45–60 minutes. This time allows the top to firm up and form a skin, which helps the macarons rise up and form their trademark ruffly 'feet'. Do not let them sit out for longer than they need to because they could begin to deflate.

7. Meanwhile, make the lemon curd. Put the lemon juice, caster sugar, egg and egg yolks into a medium heatproof bowl and set the bowl over a saucepan of gently simmering water, making sure the water doesn't touch the bottom of the bowl. Whisk constantly with an electric whisk until the mix is light and fluffy and begins to thicken to the consistency of custard. This will take about 10 minutes. Remove the saucepan from the heat, with the bowl of curd on top, and whisk in the butter, cube by cube, until it is all incorporated. Pass the curd through a fine sieve into a clean bowl, cover the surface of the curd with clingfilm (to prevent a skin forming) and chill.

8. Meanwhile, preheat the oven to 180°C/160°C fan/gas 4.

9. Bake the macaron shells for 13–15 minutes – to test if they are done, lightly touch the top of a macaron with a spoon or your finger (careful, it's hot). If the macaron seems wobbly, it needs another 1–2 minutes; if it seems set, it's done.

10. Let the shells cool on the baking sheet for 15 minutes, then transfer to a wire rack to continue cooling. If the macaron shells stick to the baking parchment, let them cool on the baking sheet a little longer before removing.

11. Once the macaron shells have fully cooled, they can be filled. Spread half the macaron shells with lemon curd and then sandwich together with their other halves.

Pears Belle Hélène with Chocolate Orange Sauce

This is a dessert of pears that have been poached in a sugar syrup flavoured with vanilla and various spices, then served with a chocolate sauce. In this recipe I've added orange to the sauce because it's one of my favourite flavour combinations. This is a really classic French dessert that's perfect for dinner parties. Not only is it a delicious end to a meal, but you can make all the elements ahead of time and plate it up just when you're ready to serve.

SERVES: 4
PREP TIME: 20 MINUTES
COOKING TIME: ABOUT 30 MINUTES, PLUS 2 HOURS COOLING

FOR THE PEARS
200g caster sugar
2 star anise
1 cinnamon stick
4 cardamon pods, cracked
1 vanilla pod, split lengthways
juice of 1 lemon
4 firm but ripe pears such as Williams or Comice, peeled, halved and cored

FOR THE CHOCOLATE ORANGE SAUCE
200ml double cream
2 tbsp honey
40g butter
grated zest and juice of 1 orange
2 tbsp Cointreau
100g dark chocolate (70% cocoa solids), chopped

TO SERVE
crème fraîche
30g flaked almonds, toasted
grated orange zest

1. First poach the pears. Put the caster sugar and 500ml of cold water into a medium saucepan. Add the star anise, cinnamon stick, cardamon, vanilla pod and lemon juice and bring to the boil, then reduce the heat and allow to infuse for a few minutes, stirring occasionally until the sugar has dissolved.

2. Add the pear halves to the poaching syrup and cover with a circle of baking parchment to keep them submerged. Poach gently for 20 minutes until softened but still holding their shape, making sure you don't overcook them. Turn off the heat and allow the pears to cool in the liquor, for at least 2 hours.

3. To make the chocolate orange sauce, pour the cream into a small saucepan. Add the honey, butter, orange zest and juice and Cointreau. Heat gently until it almost reaches boiling point, then remove from the heat.

4. Put the chocolate into a large bowl and pour the hot orange-infused cream over it. Leave to sit for a couple of minutes to melt the chocolate, then whisk together until smooth. Allow to cool for 5–10 minutes to thicken a little.

5. Remove the pears from the syrup using a slotted spoon and arrange on serving plates. Serve a scoop of crème fraîche alongside and drizzle the chocolate orange sauce on top of the pears. Scatter with the flaked almonds and a little orange zest to serve.

Family

Holidays

For me family holidays in France bring back so many happy memories from when my children were young. We'd hire a house in Grimaud, Nice or Antibes and our first stop as soon as we arrived would always be the local market to stock up on ingredients. I love French markets! Stall after stall of incredible produce, from fresh fruit and vegetables to locally made cheeses and charcuterie. There's usually a butcher and a fishmonger too. I would fill bags and baskets with the most beautiful-looking tomatoes, olives, breads, fresh mussels and peppery saucisson. Then my brain would get to work dreaming up all the delicious French meals I was going to cook for my family. Sometimes they'd request a little taste of home, so I'd put a French spin on an old family favourite like sausage and mash! And if I wasn't on dinner duty, we'd go to a local brasserie for a bite to eat. This is where I first discovered dishes like cassoulet, veal steak with chips and a real favourite of mine, niçoise salad. In my experience brasseries always serve simple, delicious food. They don't often stray from the classics, but they always get them right.

In this chapter I have recreated some of those brasserie dishes with my own twist and included some memorable meals that I cooked with my market produce for Jane and the kids. Of course you don't have to be on holiday to make any of these recipes, but I hope they'll bring some sunshine into your kitchen.

Leek and Goats' Cheese on Toast

Pepper Salad on Toast with White Bean Purée

Crab, Lemon and Chilli Toasts with Spiced Crab Pâté

Tuna Niçoise Salad

Charred Watermelon Salad with Quick Radish Pickle,
Roquefort and Walnuts

French Chop Chop Salad with Brioche Croutons

Grilled Asparagus with Goats' Cheese and Shallot
and Almond Vinaigrette

Chilled Tomato Soup with Remoulade on Toast

Lamb Chops with Roast Pumpkin, Black Olive
and Anchovy

Scallops with Lentils

Spiced Saucisson Baked Eggs with Creamy Spinach
and Garlic

Sausages with French Onion Sauce and Roasted
New Potatoes

Cassoulet

Pork Chops with Green Olive Sauce

Côte de Veau with Chips and Roasted Garlic
Mayonnaise

Leek and Goats' Cheese on Toast

This is a bit of a cross between a French croque monsieur, a Welsh rarebit and posh cheese on toast. Leeks take on the most divine flavour when charred and are perfect piled onto toast, topped with a creamy, double cheese sauce and grilled until golden and bubbly. Absolute heaven and perfect for brunch, lunch or dinner with a crisp and crunchy salad on the side. But beware, these are seriously moreish so you may need to double the recipe!

SERVES: 4
PREP TIME: 20 MINUTES
COOKING TIME: ABOUT 25 MINUTES

2 leeks, washed and trimmed

olive oil, for drizzling

30g butter

1 tbsp Dijon or wholegrain mustard

2 tbsp Worcestershire sauce

30g plain flour

125ml good-quality chicken stock

100g Cheddar cheese, grated

100g soft goats' cheese, crumbled

4 slices of bread, such as sourdough

sea salt and freshly ground black pepper

FOR THE SALAD

3 tbsp extra virgin olive oil

1 tbsp red wine vinegar

1 heaped tsp Dijon or wholegrain mustard

pinch of caster sugar

75g lamb's lettuce

2 little gem lettuces, leaves separated and torn if large

25g goats' cheese

75g toasted hazelnuts, chopped

1. Preheat the grill to medium-high. Cut the leeks in half lengthways, drizzle with olive oil and season with salt and pepper, then grill on a baking tray for 10 minutes, turning frequently, or until charred all over and softened. Thinly slice and set aside.

2. Melt the butter, Dijon mustard and Worcestershire sauce together in a saucepan over medium heat. Stir in the flour and cook for about 1 minute to get rid of the floury taste, but avoid letting it brown. Whisk in the stock and cook for a further 3–4 minutes until it becomes a smooth, thick paste. Whisk in both cheeses until melted. Set aside to cool while you make the salad.

3. For the salad, pour the extra virgin olive oil, vinegar, Dijon mustard, a pinch of sugar and some salt and pepper into a jar, seal the lid and shake until it is combined. Arrange the salad leaves in a large bowl, drizzle the dressing over the top, then crumble over the goats' cheese and chopped hazelnuts.

4. Preheat the grill and gently toast the bread slices on both sides. Cover each slice with the sliced leeks and divide the sauce among the four slices. Place on a baking tray and put under the grill for 4–5 minutes until golden and bubbling. Serve with the salad.

Pepper Salad on Toast with White Bean Purée

These make a fabulous lunch, starter or snack at any time of the day. The toasted bread is topped with a smooth and creamy white bean purée, adorned with a red pepper salad and finished off with pistou, something I discovered in Provence. It's a basil sauce, like pesto, but much simpler with just olive oil and garlic added to it.

SERVES: 4
PREP TIME: 20 MINUTES
COOKING TIME: 20 MINUTES

FOR THE PISTOU SAUCE
50g fresh basil
3 garlic cloves
7 tbsp extra virgin olive oil

FOR THE WHITE BEAN PURÉE
300g white beans (tinned or from a jar), drained and rinsed
2 tbsp olive oil
juice of ½ lemon
½ red chilli, deseeded and finely diced
1 slice of crustless bread (optional)
pinch of salt

FOR THE PEPPER SALAD
2 red peppers
2 tbsp olive oil, plus extra for drizzling
2 shallots, thinly sliced
2 fresh heritage tomatoes, diced
splash of white wine vinegar
handful of fresh basil leaves, torn
sea salt and freshly ground black pepper

TO SERVE
4 slices of white sourdough bread

1. Put all the pistou sauce ingredients in a blender or food processor, add a little salt and pepper and blitz until smooth. Transfer to a bowl and set aside.

2. Put the white bean purée ingredients into a blender or food processor and blend until smooth but still retaining some texture. You can add a chunk of crustless bread to the mix if you'd like your purée to be thicker. Pour into a bowl and set aside.

3. Drizzle the whole red peppers with oil, then put directly onto a griddle pan over high heat to char and soften, turning often. This will take about 10 minutes. If using a barbecue, place the red peppers directly onto the coals to char.

4. Meanwhile, heat the olive oil in a frying pan and gently fry the shallots with a little salt and pepper over low-medium heat for 3–4 minutes, or until soft.

5. Put the grilled peppers into a bowl, cover with clingfilm and leave to cool for 10 minutes – this will make it easier to remove the skin.

6. Slip the skin off the peppers and then dice and add to a bowl. Add the tomato, the cooked shallots, a pinch of salt and pepper, the white wine vinegar, a glug of olive oil and the basil and mix together.

7. Char or toast the bread on a griddle pan, then spread a generous spoonful of white bean purée on top. Add a tablespoon of the pepper salad, then top with the pistou and serve.

MARCUS'S TIP

These would make great canapés at a party – just cut the toasts into small bite-size pieces.

Crab, Lemon and Chilli Toasts with Spiced Crab Pâté

My wife Jane absolutely loves crab so this is exactly the sort of thing I make for relaxed, sunny lunches together, especially when we're on holiday by the coast. The brown crab meat is perfect for making an easy pâté to spread on crusty bread, topped with the sweeter white meat in a fresh, summery dressing.

SERVES: 4 AS A LIGHT LUNCH OR STARTER
PREP TIME: 15–20 MINUTES

FOR THE BROWN CRAB PÂTÉ
200g brown crab meat
few drops of fish sauce
few drops of Worcestershire sauce
1 garlic clove, chopped
1 slice of white bread, crusts removed
grated zest of ½ lemon
pinch of cayenne pepper
sea salt and freshly ground black pepper

FOR THE WHITE CRAB
200g fresh white crab meat, picked
grated zest of ½ lemon and a squeeze of juice
1 small red chilli, deseeded and finely chopped
2 spring onions, finely chopped
2 tbsp fresh chopped herbs, such as coriander, chives, parsley or tarragon
pinch of cayenne pepper

TO SERVE
small baguette, cut into 8 slices on the diagonal, toasted
watercress
pinch of cayenne pepper
lemon zest, to finish

1. To make the crab pâté, place the brown crab meat in a blender, add the fish sauce, Worcestershire sauce and garlic and blend until smooth. Tear in the bread, add the lemon zest, cayenne pepper and salt and pepper to taste, then blend to a paste; it should have a smooth, spreadable consistency. Spoon into a bowl, cover, and refrigerate until needed.

2. Place the white crab meat into a separate bowl, add the lemon zest, a good squeeze of juice, the chilli, spring onions, herbs and a pinch of cayenne pepper. Stir together and season well with salt and pepper to taste.

3. To serve, spread the brown crab pâté evenly onto the toasted baguette slices. Arrange the toasts on a serving platter or board and top each with the white crab meat mixture.

4. Finish each toast with some watercress, a pinch of cayenne and a touch more lemon zest, to serve.

Tuna Niçoise Salad

I love all the different elements that go into a niçoise salad: boiled eggs, olives, green beans, tuna, potatoes – it's packed full of beautiful ingredients and somehow manages to be both light and filling at the same time. Traditionally the potatoes are simply boiled, but for a bit of a treat I've roasted mine, adding extra crunch and richness. You could use seared fresh tuna steaks instead of tinned if you wanted to go all out.

SERVES: 4
PREP TIME: 15 MINUTES
COOKING TIME: ABOUT 30 MINUTES

16 small new potatoes (approx. 600g)

2 tbsp olive oil

1 tsp herbes de Provence

100g green beans, trimmed and cut in half

4 eggs

1 romaine lettuce, leaves torn

4 vine tomatoes, cut into wedges

100g black olives, pitted

2 x 160g tins good-quality tuna, drained

8 anchovy fillets in oil, sliced in half lengthways

1 tbsp baby capers

sea salt and freshly ground black pepper

FOR THE DRESSING

1 tbsp white wine vinegar

1 tsp Dijon mustard

1 garlic clove, crushed

drizzle of honey

75ml extra virgin olive oil

1. Preheat the oven to 220°C/200°C fan/gas 7.

2. Bring a medium saucepan of salted water to the boil. Add the potatoes and cook for 8–10 minutes until tender. Drain and allow to steam dry. Cut any large potatoes in half.

3. Pour 2 tablespoons of olive oil into a roasting tin. Heat in the oven for 5 minutes until hot, then add the potatoes, sprinkle in the herbes de Provence and a good pinch of salt and toss to coat. Roast in the oven for about 15–20 minutes until golden brown and crisp.

4. Meanwhile, bring a small saucepan of salted water to the boil and add the green beans. Cook for 2–3 minutes until tender, then plunge into a bowl of iced water and drain.

5. Bring a saucepan of water to a simmer and add the eggs. Cook for 7 minutes, then remove from the heat and plunge into iced water. When cool, peel and cut into halves or quarters.

6. To assemble the salad, scatter the lettuce onto a large serving platter. Top with the tomato wedges and black olives, then flake over the tuna and arrange the anchovies on top. Add the potatoes and green beans to the platter and scatter with the baby capers.

7. To make the dressing, whisk the vinegar, Dijon mustard, garlic, honey and salt and pepper in a bowl. Gradually whisk in the oil until combined and thickened.

8. Drizzle the dressing over the salad and gently toss together. Arrange the eggs on top and serve.

Charred Watermelon Salad with Quick Radish Pickle, Roquefort and Walnuts

Whenever I go on a French summer holiday one of the first things we buy is a huge watermelon. I used to love handing my kids big wedges to get stuck into when they were young, the juice running down their chins. These days I often use it in savoury salads. If you've never tried charred watermelon you're in for such a treat; the natural sugars in the fruit caramelise and take on amazing depth of flavour.

SERVES: 4–6
PREP TIME: 15 MINUTES, PLUS 30 MINUTES PICKLING
COOKING TIME: 10–15 MINUTES

½ small watermelon (approx. 1.2kg)

olive oil, for drizzling

½ cucumber, halved lengthways

100g Roquefort cheese

50g walnut halves, toasted and roughly chopped

sea salt and freshly ground black pepper

grated lemon zest, to finish

FOR THE QUICK RADISH AND SHALLOT PICKLE
6 tbsp red wine vinegar

2 tbsp caster sugar

pinch of dried chilli flakes

12 round mixed radishes (150–200g), thinly sliced

1 banana shallot, thinly sliced

FOR THE DRESSING
75ml extra virgin olive oil

juice of ½ lemon

1 tbsp reserved liquor from the radish and shallot pickle

1 tsp honey

small handful of fresh mint leaves, shredded

1. First prepare the radish and shallot pickle. Mix the red wine vinegar, caster sugar and chilli flakes together in a bowl. Add the radishes and shallot and mix together. Allow to stand for at least 30 minutes. (Once pickled, reserve some of the liquor to make the dressing.)

2. Cut the watermelon in half lengthways to make 2 large wedges. Remove the rind and skin and then cut the flesh into 2cm slices, removing any large seeds. Pat the slices dry with kitchen paper and drizzle both sides of each slice with a little olive oil and some salt and pepper.

3. Place a griddle pan over high heat until almost smoking hot. Add the watermelon slices and griddle for 2–3 minutes on each side, cooking in batches until nicely charred. Remove from the heat and continue with the remaining slices.

4. Meanwhile, cut the cucumber into slices on the diagonal.

5. To make the dressing, whisk the extra virgin olive oil, lemon juice, reserved pickling liquor, honey and some seasoning together in a small bowl until combined. Stir through the shredded mint.

6. Arrange the charred watermelon onto individual serving plates or a large platter. Scatter the cucumber slices over, followed by the pickled radish and shallot. Crumble the Roquefort into bite-size pieces and arrange on top, then scatter over the walnuts.

7. Drizzle the dressing over the salad and finely grate a little lemon zest over to finish.

French Chop Chop Salad with Brioche Croutons

I can't get enough of chop chop salads. They can be made with any ingredients you like, including meats and cheeses, and are a great way of using up what's left in your fridge. Just chop everything up to roughly the same size, add a tasty dressing and you've got yourself a quick and easy meal. In this recipe I've used all my favourite French produce: charcuterie, Brie and olives with brioche croutons.

SERVES: 4–6
PREP TIME: 20 MINUTES
COOKING TIME: 5 MINUTES

1 frisee lettuce, leaves separated

1 red pepper, deseeded and sliced

4 vine or heritage tomatoes, cut into small wedges

½ cucumber, sliced

1 banana shallot, thinly sliced

100g black olives, pitted

200g selection of French charcuterie such as saucisson, sliced or diced

160g Brie, cut into chunks (make sure it's not overly ripe)

sea salt and freshly ground black pepper

FOR THE ORANGE DRESSING
75ml extra virgin olive oil

1 tbsp white wine vinegar

grated zest and juice of 1 orange

2 tsp wholegrain mustard

1 tbsp honey

FOR THE CROUTONS
100g brioche loaf, cut or torn into bite-size pieces

4–6 tbsp olive oil, plus extra for frying

2 tsp herbes de Provence (or dried mixed herbs)

1. First make the croutons. Place the brioche pieces into a large bowl with the olive oil, herbes de Provence and some salt and pepper and toss together to evenly coat. Add a drizzle of oil to a large non-stick frying pan and fry the croutons (in batches if necessary) for 4–5 minutes, turning frequently, until evenly toasted. Remove from the heat and set aside.

2. To make the orange dressing, whisk the extra virgin olive oil, vinegar, orange zest and juice, mustard, honey and seasoning together until combined.

3. Place the frisee lettuce, red pepper, tomatoes, cucumber and shallot together in a very large bowl. Add the olives, charcuterie, chunks of Brie and season well with salt and pepper. Mix together and pour in the dressing to coat.

4. Transfer to a large serving platter and scatter the croutons over the top to serve.

Grilled Asparagus with Goats' Cheese and Shallot and Almond Vinaigrette

I love grilled asparagus served with a warm vinaigrette; it's such an elegant dish that you can eat as a main course for a light supper, or as a side to steak or fish. A classic French vinaigrette is one part vinegar to three parts oil with mustard, salt and pepper. I use that as a blueprint for so many recipes and then think of ways to change it up. The addition here of shallots, capers, honey and almonds makes it really special.

SERVES: 4
PREP TIME: 10 MINUTES
COOKING TIME: ABOUT 15 MINUTES

2 bunches of asparagus, trimmed

olive oil, for drizzling

handful of wild rocket

50g hard goats' cheese

sea salt and freshly ground black pepper

grated lemon zest, to serve

FOR THE SHALLOT AND ALMOND VINAIGRETTE

75ml extra virgin olive oil

1 shallot, finely chopped

2 tbsp white wine vinegar

1 tbsp capers, chopped

1 tsp Dijon mustard

1 tsp wholegrain mustard

3–4 sprigs of fresh thyme, leaves picked and chopped

1 tbsp honey

50g toasted whole blanched almonds, roughly chopped

1. Bring a saucepan of salted water to the boil and blanch the asparagus for 2 minutes, then drain. Dry well on a tray lined with kitchen paper, then drizzle with olive oil and season well with salt and pepper.

2. Heat a large griddle pan until hot and add the asparagus in batches, cooking over high heat for 1–2 minutes and turning a couple of times until nicely charred.

3. To make the vinaigrette, heat 1 tablespoon of the oil in a small saucepan, add the shallot and cook for a few minutes over low-medium heat to soften without colouring. Gradually add the rest of the oil, then stir in the vinegar, capers, mustards, thyme and honey. Season with salt and pepper and warm gently for a couple of minutes. Stir in the chopped almonds and remove from the heat.

4. Divide the asparagus between serving plates and top each with a little wild rocket. Finely grate over the goats' cheese (or use a vegetable peeler to create shavings), followed by a little lemon zest. Finish with a good drizzle of the shallot and almond vinaigrette to serve.

Chilled Tomato Soup with Remoulade on Toast

My wife adores cold soups so I've made many different versions of this recipe over the years. It's one of the first things we eat as a family when we go on holiday, after we've been to the market to buy ripe, local tomatoes. I'm always looking for new things to serve alongside it and remoulade is the perfect accompaniment. It's creamy, sharp and crunchy, which is exactly what the smooth, sweet and tangy soup needs.

SERVES: 4
PREP TIME: 30 MINUTES
COOKING TIME: ABOUT 5 MINUTES

6 large, ripe assorted tomatoes, chopped

100ml tomato juice

1 tbsp tomato purée

1 tsp smoked paprika

30g flaked almonds, toasted

1 tbsp sherry vinegar

1 tbsp olive oil

4 thick slices of white bread, crusts removed

small bunch of fresh basil, leaves chopped

ice cubes

sea salt and freshly ground black pepper

FOR THE REMOULADE ON TOAST
¼ small celeriac

grated zest and juice of ½ lemon

½ tsp wholegrain mustard

3 tbsp good-quality mayonnaise

1 tbsp finely chopped fresh flat-leaf parsley

4 slices of sourdough bread

extra virgin olive oil, for drizzling

1. Add the chopped tomatoes to a large bowl along with a generous amount of seasoning. Add the tomato juice, tomato purée, smoked paprika and toasted flaked almonds and mix together, then add the sherry vinegar and a tablespoon of the olive oil. Tear the bread slices into pieces and add to the bowl along with the basil leaves and a tablespoon of oil. Mix together well.

2. Transfer the tomato mixture to a blender (in batches) and blitz until smooth, adding a little splash of water and a couple of ice cubes to each batch to chill. Blend again until smooth. Transfer to a large serving bowl and keep chilled.

3. While the soup chills in the fridge, make the celeriac remoulade. Peel the celeriac and thinly slice into matchsticks, then toss into a bowl with the lemon zest and juice and some salt. Leave to sit for 5 minutes, then add the mustard, mayonnaise, parsley and a pinch of black pepper and mix well.

4. Drizzle a little oil over the sourdough slices and then griddle on a hot griddle pan until lightly charred on both sides. Repeat until all the toast is ready. Place a generous spoonful of celeriac remoulade onto each slice of hot griddled toast. Spoon the chilled soup into four bowls, drizzle with a little extra virgin olive oil and freshly ground black pepper and serve with the remoulade toast alongside.

Lamb Chops with Roast Pumpkin, Black Olive and Anchovy

Marinating lamb chops for days isn't strictly necessary so if you haven't got time, don't let that stop you making this recipe. But if you can plan ahead, marinating helps the flavour of the herbs to deeply penetrate the meat and the result is sublime. I love serving lamb with a punchy, flavourful vinaigrette for a light, but really satisfying supper. Photographed overleaf.

SERVES: 4
PREP TIME: 45 MINUTES,
PLUS 24–48 HOURS MARINATING
COOKING TIME: ABOUT 45 MINUTES

2 French-trimmed lamb racks, each with 6 bones, cut into chops

150ml olive oil, plus 2 tbsp for searing

3 sprigs of fresh rosemary

3 sprigs of fresh thyme

sea salt and freshly ground black pepper

chopped fresh parsley, to serve

FOR THE ROASTED PUMPKIN

850g pumpkin, deseeded and cut into chunks

2 tbsp olive oil

2 sprigs of fresh rosemary, leaves chopped

4 garlic cloves, unpeeled

FOR THE VINAIGRETTE

2 tbsp extra virgin olive oil

1 tbsp sherry vinegar

1 tsp lemon juice

50g anchovy fillets, cut into 1cm pieces

50g pitted black olives, sliced into strips

1. Put the lamb chops in a bowl or strong freezer bag and pour over 150ml olive oil. Add the rosemary and thyme sprigs and leave to marinate for 24–48 hours, turning the lamb over every so often.

2. Now roast the pumpkin. Preheat the oven to 200°C/180°C fan/gas 6. Place the pumpkin chunks into a shallow roasting tray, drizzle with the olive oil and scatter over the chopped rosemary and garlic cloves. Season with salt and pepper and roast for 30–35 minutes, or until golden all over and tender.

3. Increase the oven temperature to 220°C/200°C fan/gas 7.

4. To cook the lamb chops, heat 2 tablespoons of olive oil in a griddle pan over high heat. Remove the lamb from the marinade and season with salt and pepper. Add to the hot pan and sear well on each side. Put in the oven and cook for a further 5–10 minutes, depending on how you like your lamb cooked: 5 minutes will give you rare lamb and 10 minutes medium-well done. Remove from the oven and leave to rest for 15 minutes.

5. While the lamb rests, mix together the extra virgin olive oil, sherry vinegar, lemon juice, anchovies and olives for the vinaigrette.

6. To assemble, spoon the roasted pumpkin onto plates and arrange the chops on top. Spoon over the vinaigrette, scatter with a little chopped parsley and serve.

MARCUS'S TIP

Sometimes if I want to impress, I'll serve this recipe as a rack of lamb instead of individual chops. Skip the marinade stage, set the oven to 220°C/200°C fan/gas 7 and season the rack of lamb well. Add olive oil to a frying pan and when hot, sear the lamb well on all sides until nice and brown. Transfer to a tray and roast in the oven for 15 minutes for rare, 20 for medium. Remove and rest before carving at the table.

Scallops with Lentils

This is hands down my favourite way to cook lentils. My whole family loves it too, whether we're at home or away. They're rich and flavourful with a lovely warmth from the smoked paprika. I've made several versions of this dish over the years with cod and mascarpone, even sausages. No matter how I change it up, it never disappoints and adding scallops has been a bit of a revelation, making humble lentils something really special.

SERVES: 4
PREP TIME: 10 MINUTES
COOKING TIME: ABOUT 45 MINUTES

12–16 scallops (3–4 per person, depending on size)

2 tbsp olive oil

2 onions, thinly sliced

1 garlic clove, crushed

1 tsp sweet smoked paprika

2 tbsp tomato purée

250ml tomato juice

600ml good-quality chicken or vegetable stock

250g yellow lentils, well rinsed (I used mung dal)

1 tbsp olive oil

grated zest of ½ lemon

½ bunch of fresh basil, leaves picked

sea salt and freshly ground black pepper

1. Prepare the scallops by removing and discarding the roe. Set aside.

2. Preheat the oven to 200°C/180°C fan/gas 6.

3. Heat the olive oil in a large ovenproof casserole dish over medium heat. Add the onions, season well with salt and pepper and cook for about 10 minutes until soft, then add the garlic and cook for a further 3 minutes. Stir in the smoked paprika, followed by the tomato purée. Cook for 1 minute, then mix in the tomato juice and stock. Season again with salt and pepper and bring to the boil.

4. Add the lentils, mix well, cover the casserole dish with a lid (or foil) and place in the oven for 20 minutes, stirring after 10 minutes.

5. Remove the casserole from the oven and remove the lid or foil. Season the scallops and add them to the lentils, pressing them down with a spoon so they are almost submerged. Drizzle the olive oil on top of the scallops, then pop the lid (or foil) back on top and return the casserole to the oven for 6 minutes.

6. Sprinkle with lemon zest and basil leaves and serve immediately.

MARCUS'S TIP

Make sure everyone is at the table ready to eat when you take this out of the oven. The hot lentils will continue to cook the scallops even outside of the oven, so you want to make sure you serve it right away to avoid the scallops getting overcooked.

Spiced Saucisson Baked Eggs with Creamy Spinach and Garlic

Baked eggs in a creamy roux-based sauce make the most delicious and indulgent breakfast or brunch, especially when you're on holiday or at the weekend. This recipe, with lots of spinach, saucisson, garlic and Gruyère is seriously good. I like to make these baked eggs in individual ramekins so there's no arguing over who's got the most sauce, but you can just as easily make it in one big dish for everyone to dig in. Photographed overleaf.

SERVES: 4
PREP TIME: 20–25 MINUTES
COOKING TIME: ABOUT 25 MINUTES

2 tbsp olive oil, plus extra for drizzling

2 small banana shallots, thinly sliced

4 garlic cloves, crushed

3–4 sprigs of fresh thyme, leaves picked

80g saucisson, roughly chopped

200g baby spinach

4 eggs

30g Gruyère cheese, finely grated

FOR THE BÉCHAMEL SAUCE
200ml milk

30g butter

30g plain flour

2 tsp Dijon mustard

freshly grated nutmeg

100g crème fraîche

sea salt and freshly ground black pepper

TO SERVE
crusty baguette

small handful of chopped fresh flat-leaf parsley (optional)

1. Preheat the oven to 200°C/180°C fan/gas 6.

2. Firstly, make the creamy béchamel sauce. Heat the milk in a small saucepan until almost boiling, then turn off the heat. Melt the butter in a separate saucepan over low heat and whisk in the flour. Cook for 1–2 minutes, stirring continuously until thickened. Gradually whisk in half the hot milk, stirring to combine, then whisk in the remaining milk. Cook for a minute or two, stirring until thickened, then remove from the heat. Season well with salt and pepper and whisk in the Dijon mustard and freshly grated nutmeg. Allow to cool for a minute before stirring in the crème fraîche.

3. Heat the olive oil in a large sauté or frying pan over medium heat. Add the shallots, season with salt and pepper and cook for 2–3 minutes to soften. Stir in the garlic, thyme leaves and saucisson and cook for another 2–3 minutes. Stir in the spinach and cook, stirring, for about 2 minutes until wilted.

4. Spoon the spinach and saucisson mixture into the béchamel sauce and mix together. Transfer to four individual serving or gratin dishes (around 16cm round by 3cm deep, or approx. 250–270ml capacity). Use the back of a spoon to make four dips in the creamed spinach. Crack an egg into each dip, then sprinkle the grated Gruyère over and drizzle with a little olive oil.

5. Bake in the oven for 12–13 minutes until the egg whites are just set and the yolks are still soft and cooked to your liking. Sprinkle with parsley (if using), and serve immediately.

Sausages with French Onion Sauce and Roasted New Potatoes

Sometimes when you're travelling, you crave a little taste of home and that is exactly how this recipe came about; it's my holiday take on bangers and mash. I've given the classic gravy a little upgrade and packed it full of different varieties of onion, including pickled for a bit of tang, and swapped the mash for roasted new potatoes. It's equally satisfying as the Great British original, but with a little *je ne sais quoi*!

SERVES: 4
PREP TIME: 20 MINUTES
COOKING TIME: ABOUT 50 MINUTES

400g new potatoes

2 tbsp butter

1 red onion, thinly sliced

2 spring onions, thinly sliced

handful of pickled onions, chopped

2 tbsp chopped fresh thyme leaves

1 tbsp plain flour

100ml red wine

550ml good-quality chicken stock

1 tbsp Dijon mustard

1 tsp Worcestershire sauce

2 tbsp olive oil

8 large pork sausages

chopped fresh parsley, to finish

sea salt and freshly ground black pepper

1. Fill a saucepan with water, season with a tablespoon of salt and add the potatoes. Bring to a simmer and cook for 10–15 minutes until the potatoes are soft. Drain and allow to cool. When cool enough to handle, slice the potatoes into 1cm discs. Set them to one side.

2. Melt the butter in a saucepan and add the onions, salt and pepper and thyme and gently fry for 10 minutes until soft and starting to caramelise. Stir in the flour and cook for 2 minutes, then deglaze the pan with the wine and cook until the volume of liquid has reduced by half.

3. Add the stock and bring to the boil, stirring all the time until you have a thick sauce – this will take about 10 minutes. Add the Dijon mustard, Worcestershire sauce and salt and pepper to taste. Set aside while you cook the sausages and potatoes.

4. Preheat the grill to medium.

5. Heat the olive oil in a large heavy-based frying pan over high heat, carefully place the potato slices into the pan and turn every couple of minutes until golden on both sides. Repeat until all are cooked and crispy. Season with a generous pinch of salt.

6. While the potatoes are cooking, grill the sausages for 15–20 minutes, turning frequently, until cooked through.

7. Serve the sausages and crispy potatoes with the gravy poured over the top and a sprinkling of parsley.

Cassoulet

This is a wonderful hearty and meaty bean stew from southern France. It's extremely satisfying to make from scratch using my confit duck leg recipe on page 39. Having said that, it's easily adaptable to suit your taste so you can use chicken if you prefer or even make a version with just sausages.

SERVES: 6
PREP TIME: 20–25 MINUTES,
PLUS OVERNIGHT SOAKING
COOKING TIME: 3 HOURS 15
MINUTES–3 HOURS 45 MINUTES

300g dried haricot beans
1 onion, halved
1 whole garlic bulb
sprigs of fresh thyme, parsley and rosemary and 2 bay leaves tied together with string
1 unsmoked ham hock
2 tbsp goose or duck fat
500g pork belly, cubed
4 Toulouse sausages
4 confit duck legs (page 39)
1 large onion, thinly sliced
1 large carrot, diced
1 celery stick, sliced

TO FINISH
2 tbsp duck fat
3–4 tbsp dried white breadcrumbs
3 tbsp chopped fresh flat-leaf parsley
green salad, to serve

1. Place the beans into a large bowl, cover with cold water and soak overnight. Drain the beans well and put them in a large ovenproof casserole dish. Pour in cold fresh water until it comes about 3cm above the top of the beans, then add the halved onion, garlic bulb, tied herb bundle and ham hock. Bring to the boil, then cover and simmer for about 1½–2 hours, or until the beans are just tender but not falling apart and the ham hock is falling away from the bone.

2. Meanwhile, heat 1 tablespoon of the duck fat in a frying pan and fry the pork belly cubes, until crisp and golden; remove from the pan and set aside. Repeat with the sausages and then the confit duck legs. When cool, cut the sausages into large chunks and strip the meat from the confit duck legs in large pieces.

3. Remove the ham hock and, when cool enough to handle, strip the meat from it, discarding the fat and bone. Squeeze the garlic cloves from their skins and discard the skins. Discard the onions and herbs. Preheat the oven to 140°C/120°C fan/gas 1.

4. Drain the beans, reserving the liquid. Heat a tablespoon of duck fat in the casserole dish, add the sliced onion, carrot and celery and fry over medium heat for 5–6 minutes, or until softened. Tip in the beans, the squeezed garlic and the pieces of cooked meat and sausage. Mix well, then top with just enough liquid to cover. You probably won't need to add any seasoning, as both the ham and the confit will be quite salty.

5. Place the casserole dish in the oven and bake for 1½ hours, or until everything is tender.

6. Just before you are ready to serve, heat the 2 tablespoons of duck fat in a frying pan and fry the breadcrumbs very briefly until golden. Scatter the breadcrumbs over the top, followed by the parsley. Serve with a green salad.

Pork Chops with Green Olive Sauce

This green olive sauce was inspired by the hundreds, if not thousands, of spectacular olive groves I've driven past in Provence. I think they're the most beautiful trees and I even have a few growing in my back garden in London. The thing I love most about the sauce is that it's so versatile too. I serve it with sardines on toast, simple grilled white fish, steak sandwiches – you name it – but it is especially good with a beautifully grilled pork chop.

SERVES: 4
PREP TIME: 20 MINUTES,
PLUS RESTING
COOKING TIME: 30 MINUTES

2 tbsp fennel seeds

2 tbsp black peppercorns

2 tbsp sea salt flakes

1 tbsp fresh thyme leaves

3 tbsp soft light brown sugar

1 x 4-bone pork loin rack (best end), sliced into 4 chops

olive oil, for drizzling

FOR THE GREEN OLIVE SAUCE

200g pitted green olives

200ml warm chicken stock

50ml extra virgin olive oil

1 slice of white bread, crust removed and torn into pieces

1 garlic clove, roughly chopped

juice of ½ lemon

sea salt

1. Preheat the oven to 180°C/160°C fan/gas 4.

2. Toast the fennel seeds in a dry frying pan over medium heat, then add to a pestle and mortar, along with the peppercorns and salt, and grind to a fine powder. Stir through the thyme and sugar.

3. Score the fat on the pork chops, then season the pork with the spice mix and drizzle with a little olive oil.

4. Place a frying pan over high heat; when hot, add the chops and sear on both sides (you may want to do this in two batches). Transfer the chops to a roasting tray and roast in the oven for 15–20 minutes until the meat feels firm to the touch. Set aside to rest for at least 10 minutes.

5. To make the olive sauce, put all the ingredients apart from the lemon juice into a high-speed blender and blitz for 1–2 minutes until smooth. Add the lemon juice and season with salt to taste.

6. Serve the chops with the olive sauce and any resting juices spooned over the meat.

Côte de Veau with Chips and Roasted Garlic Mayonnaise

This is a version of steak frites that I always order when I see it on a bistro menu. I've added roasted garlic to the mayonnaise, which takes away the harshness of raw garlic and adds a really delicious sweetness that works so well with veal – and chips of course! If you're not up for making your own mayonnaise, you can stir some roasted garlic into a good shop-bought mayo for a quick and easy cheat. Photographed overleaf.

SERVES: 4
PREP TIME: 15–20 MINUTES,
PLUS 1 HOUR MARINATING
COOKING TIME: ABOUT 1 HOUR
15 MINUTES

FOR THE CÔTE DE VEAU
1.4–1.5kg bone in côte de veau, French trimmed
4 garlic cloves, bashed
small handful of fresh thyme leaves
3 sprigs of fresh rosemary
small handful of fresh sage leaves
2 tbsp olive oil
2 tbsp butter
sea salt and freshly ground black pepper

FOR THE HOMEMADE CHIPS
1kg Maris Piper potatoes
3 tbsp duck fat
4–6 garlic cloves, bashed
small handful each of fresh thyme and rosemary, leaves picked and chopped

1. Place the côte de veau into a dish, season all over with salt and pepper, add the bashed garlic cloves, herbs and olive oil and leave to marinate for about 1 hour while you prepare the chips.

2. Leaving the skins on, cut the potatoes into approx. 1cm thick chips. Fill a large saucepan with salted water, add the chips, bring to the boil and then cook for 10 minutes, or until just tender. Drain in a colander and then leave to steam dry for 5 minutes in the colander. Preheat the oven to 220°C/200°C fan/gas 7.

3. Melt the duck fat in a shallow baking tray in the oven. Once it is hot, add the par cooked chips, bashed garlic cloves, thyme and rosemary. Season well and roast in the oven for 30–35 minutes, turning occasionally, or until they are golden all over.

4. When you are ready to cook the veal, place an ovenproof frying pan over high heat.

5. Remove the garlic from the marinating meat and set aside. Place the marinated côte de veau into the frying pan and sear on all sides until golden. Add the bashed garlic to the pan and then transfer to the oven to roast for 25–30 minutes. Remove the pan from the oven, add the butter and place over medium heat. Baste the meat with the melted butter and then set aside to rest.

Continued Overleaf ...

FOR THE ROASTED GARLIC MAYONNAISE

3 egg yolks

1 tbsp white wine vinegar

½ tsp Dijon mustard

225ml vegetable oil

roasted garlic cloves (from the chips)

squeeze of lemon juice

6. For the garlic mayonnaise, put the egg yolks, vinegar and Dijon mustard into a blender. With the blender on the slowest setting, slowly add the oil in a thin stream. When you have a thick mayonnaise consistency, transfer to a bowl. Squeeze the roasted garlic cloves from the chips out of their skins and mash the garlic with the back of a knife. Stir in the roasted garlic to the mayonnaise and season with salt and a squeeze of lemon juice to taste.

7. Back to the veal. Cut off each chop, remove the bone and slice. Serve the sliced côte de veau with the chips and the garlic mayonnaise on the side.

MARCUS'S TIPS

If you struggle to find veal, this recipe will work just as nicely with beef. Use either a 1.4–1.5kg bone in beef rib or 4 steaks of your choice. Simply marinate them in the same way and if you're using steaks rather than a rib skip the oven stage of the cooking process and fry them in a pan until they're cooked to your liking. If your mayo splits, try adding in a couple of drops of warm water to bring the mixture back together.

French
Cooking

at Home

This chapter is all about those easy, family-friendly, knock-out recipes that I cook at home. I want to share them with you so that you too can create delicious, crowd-pleasing French meals in your kitchen. This is the culmination of my whole life's work: from my time at catering college to the three-star Michelin restaurants where I trained to my own fine dining restaurants where I've served food in the French style to hundreds of thousands of guests. All that experience has led me to where I am in life right now. These days you'll most likely find me cooking simple recipes inspired by the food of France for myself and my family at home. I absolutely love cooking like this in my own kitchen, I find it so relaxing and enjoyable. And I take a particular pleasure from working out ways to make some of those old French recipes much easier to prepare. We don't all have the time or desire to spend hours in the kitchen, toiling away to put elaborate meals on the table.

The recipes in this chapter reflect the way my family and I like to cook and eat at home today, with simple recipes and fresh produce. Nothing that takes too much time or too many ingredients but gets everyone excited for mealtimes. I hope you'll get a real sense of enjoyment and satisfaction in creating some of these dishes for yourself and your family and that they become firm favourites in your own home too.

Tomato, Onion and Olive Tart

Bulgar Wheat Salad with Roasted Kale
and Butternut Squash

Bouillabaisse-inspired Fish Soup

Slow Roast Leg of Lamb with Mint and Caper Sauce

Fish en Papillote with Tomato and Olive Vinaigrette

Liver Lyonnaise

Braised Oxtail

Pork Chops with Fennel, Sage and Onion

Lamb Chops with Crispy Potatoes and Crème Fraîche

Madeleines

Banana Split Crêpes

Giant Rum Baba

Cherry Clafoutis

Apricot Trifle with Elderflower, White Wine
and Lavender Jelly

Tomato, Onion and Olive Tart

This is one of those dishes that will not fail to impress with how stunning it looks and delicious it tastes, but the real beauty is in how easy it is to make. There's not much cooking involved, other than caramelising the onions, and there are a few shop-bought cheats with the pastry and tapenade. Top it all off with beautifully arranged slices of tomato and you have yourself a showstopper of a tart.

SERVES: 4
PREP TIME: 20 MINUTES
COOKING TIME: ABOUT 40 MINUTES

1 x 320g sheet of ready-rolled all-butter puff pastry

1 egg, beaten

2 tbsp olive oil, plus extra for drizzling

1 large or 2 small red onions, thinly sliced

2–3 tbsp black olive tapenade

4–6 ripe tomatoes, sliced (use a mixture of sizes and colours)

2 garlic cloves, thinly sliced

handful of fresh thyme leaves

sea salt and freshly ground black pepper

salad leaves, to serve

1. Preheat the oven to 200°C/180°C fan/gas 6.

2. Put the puff pastry on baking parchment and cut out a large circle (as big as the pastry allows – you can use a dinner plate as a guide). Brush the edges with some of the beaten egg and then fold over and crimp the edges to make a rim. Use a fork to prick the base of the pastry case all over (this will prevent the pastry from puffing up too much in the oven), then brush beaten egg all over the pastry case.

3. Bake for 12–15 minutes until golden and crispy (the pastry doesn't need to be completely cooked through at this stage). Remove from the oven and set aside but leave the oven on.

4. Heat the olive oil in a medium saucepan and add the onions, salt and pepper. Fry over gentle heat for 10–15 minutes, or until softened and caramelised.

5. To assemble the tart, spread a thin layer of tapenade over the puff pastry base, followed by a generous, even layer of caramelised onions. Arrange the sliced tomatoes on top, then scatter over the garlic slices, thyme leaves, a drizzle of olive oil and salt and pepper to taste.

6. Return the tart to the oven for about 12 minutes, or until the pastry is fully cooked and the tomatoes are warmed through. Serve with a fresh salad of your choice.

Bulgar Wheat Salad with Roasted Kale and Butternut Squash

I love big, hearty salads with lots of different elements providing interesting textures and flavours. This is one of those salads that is a meal in itself, not just a side. It has got crispy kale, tender cinnamon spiced butternut squash, creamy cheese, crunchy nuts and a tangy dressing all on top of a bed of nutritious bulgar wheat. You can really make this salad your own by swapping out the veg, the cheese, the nuts or the grain; think of it as a blueprint recipe and make it work for you and your family.

SERVES: 4
PREP TIME: UNDER 30 MINUTES
COOKING TIME: ABOUT 45 MINUTES

FOR THE ROASTED BUTTERNUT SQUASH
600g butternut squash, peeled and cut into 3cm cubes

2 tbsp olive oil

1 tsp ground cinnamon, plus extra to serve

sea salt and freshly ground black pepper

FOR THE SALAD
150g kale, stalks removed and leaves roughly chopped

1 tbsp olive oil

200g bulgar wheat

400ml good-quality chicken or vegetable stock

2 spring onions, sliced

1 pomegranate, seeds only (approx. 60g)

100g feta or goats' cheese, crumbled

30g shelled pistachios, chopped

FOR THE DRESSING
3 tbsp extra virgin olive oil

2 tbsp balsamic vinegar

1. Preheat the oven to 200°C/180°C fan/gas 6.

2. Put the butternut squash into a bowl, add the 2 tablespoons olive oil and toss together with the cinnamon and some salt and pepper. Tip out onto a shallow baking tray and roast for 30 minutes, turning occasionally, or until golden all over and tender.

3. Meanwhile, put the chopped kale into a bowl and drizzle with olive oil and some salt and pepper. Massage the oil into the leaves with your hands, until the kale starts to soften, then arrange on a baking tray and roast in the oven for 6–8 minutes until the kale is crispy. Remove from the heat, season with a little more sea salt and set aside.

4. Put the bulgar wheat and stock into a saucepan and cook over medium heat for 10 minutes, or until tender and all the stock has been absorbed. Allow to steam dry for a few minutes, then fluff up the grains with a fork and arrange on a serving plate with the spring onions.

5. Top the bulgar wheat with the crispy kale and roasted squash. Add the pomegranate seeds, crumbled feta or goats' cheese and a scattering of pistachio nuts. Mix together the extra virgin olive oil and balsamic with a little salt and pepper and then drizzle over the salad. Finish with a light dusting of cinnamon.

Bouillabaisse-inspired Fish Soup

A classic bouillabaisse has a complex stock made from rock fish that can take a while to prepare. I remember one of my jobs at the restaurant where I worked in Paris was to make the bouillabaisse stock and I used to spend hours toiling away over it in a huge vat. This recipe uses ready-made fish stock, which does just as well and makes it so much easier to pull off a delicious fish soup. You can change up the fish and seafood you use depending on what you like to eat.

SERVES: 4
PREP TIME: 30 MINUTES
COOKING TIME: ABOUT 45 MINUTES

2 tbsp olive oil

½ white onion, diced

1 celery stick, finely chopped
(including leaves)

½ fennel bulb, finely chopped
(including fronds)

2 garlic cloves, crushed

2 fresh plum tomatoes, chopped

1 tsp smoked paprika

2 star anise

pinch of saffron

1–2 tbsp tomato purée

3 tbsp pastis

squeeze of lemon juice

175ml white wine

600ml fish stock

1 potato (approx. 200g), peeled and
diced

300g mussels, scrubbed and rinsed

200g salmon fillets, skin removed
and cut into chunks

200g hake fillets, skin removed and
cut into chunks

bunch of fresh flat-leaf parsley,
chopped

sea salt and freshly ground black
pepper

extra virgin olive oil, to finish

1. Heat the oil in a large sauté pan (with a lid) over medium heat, then fry the onion, celery and fennel for 10 minutes, or until softened. Add the garlic and fry for another minute, then season with salt and pepper.

2. Add the tomatoes, smoked paprika, star anise, saffron and tomato purée. Stir in and cook for 5–10 minutes until softened.

3. Add 2 tablespoons of the pastis and cook until the liquid has reduced down, then add the remaining tablespoon.

4. Add a squeeze of lemon, then pour in 100ml of the white wine and simmer for 3–4 minutes until most of the liquid has evaporated. Pour in the stock and diced potato, cover with a lid and allow to simmer for 10–15 minutes while you cook the mussels.

5. Place a saucepan over high heat. Add the mussels to the hot pan, then add the remaining 75ml wine, cover with a lid and cook for 4 minutes, or until all the shells have opened. Discard any that remain closed.

6. Add the mussel cooking liquid to the soup and remove the star anise. At this point you can take the soup off the heat and blend if you prefer a smooth soup.

7. Add the salmon and hake to the soup, along with the mussels (some in their shells, some out of their shells for texture). Simmer for 2–3 minutes, just to poach the fish until cooked.

8. Stir in the parsley, then ladle the soup into bowls, being sure to evenly distribute the hake, salmon and mussels. Drizzle with extra virgin olive oil to finish.

Slow Roast Leg of Lamb with Mint and Caper Sauce

Cooking a leg of lamb slowly at a low temperature creates pure culinary magic. The meat becomes so tender it falls off the bone and it makes its own sauce as the cooking juices mix with the herbs, onions and garlic and reduce in the roasting tray. There's a double hit of herbs, both in the rub and for the lamb to sit on, imparting so much flavour into the meat. This makes the perfect Sunday lunch, especially when served with creamy, indulgent dauphinoise potatoes!

SERVES: 6
PREP TIME: 15 MINUTES
COOKING TIME: 4 HOURS
–4 HOURS 40 MINUTES

1 leg of lamb, bone in (approx. 2kg)

6 tbsp olive oil

4 garlic cloves, crushed

4 large sprigs of fresh rosemary, leaves finely chopped

2 onions, quartered

2 garlic bulbs, halved horizontally

1 bunch of fresh rosemary

1 bunch of fresh thyme

4 bay leaves

300ml good-quality stock (chicken, lamb or vegetable)

300ml dry white wine

sea salt and freshly ground black pepper

1. Preheat the oven to 220°C/200°C fan/gas 7.

2. Using a sharp knife, make deep slits all over the lamb. In a small bowl mix the oil, garlic, chopped rosemary and a good pinch of salt and pepper. Rub evenly all over the lamb using your hands, pushing the marinade right into the meat.

3. Arrange the onion wedges and garlic bulb halves in the base of a large roasting tin, big enough to hold the lamb, to create a trivet. Scatter the bunch of rosemary and thyme over the top and add the bay leaves. Place the lamb on top of the herbs, season again generously with salt and pepper and roast in the oven for 30–40 minutes, to brown the top.

4. Reduce the oven temperature to 160°C/140°C fan/gas 3.

5. Remove the lamb from the oven and pour the stock and wine into the base of the roasting tin. Cover tightly with foil and roast in the oven for 3½–4 hours. Remove the lamb from the oven every 45 minutes or so and baste all over with the cooking juices in the tray. Add a little water to the roasting tin if needed. The lamb should be tender and starting to fall away from the bone.

FOR THE MINT AND CAPER SAUCE

2 tbsp caster sugar

4 tbsp boiling water

2 tbsp white wine vinegar

2 heaped tbsp capers, finely
chopped

small bunch of fresh mint, leaves
finely chopped

6. To make the mint and caper sauce, put the sugar into a bowl with the boiling water and stir to dissolve. Stir in the vinegar and capers and a touch of seasoning. Stir in the freshly chopped mint just before serving so it retains its vibrant green colour.

7. Remove the lamb from the oven, transfer to a serving board and cover with foil. Meanwhile, strain the cooking juices from the roasting tin through a fine sieve into a small saucepan, discarding the onions, garlic and herbs. Skim off some of the lamb fat/oil from the cooking liquor and warm gently for a few minutes to reduce slightly and intensify the flavour, until the desired consistency is reached.

8. Shred the lamb and serve with the cooking juices, mint and caper sauce and dauphinoise potatoes (see page 77).

MARCUS'S TIP

If you have any leftover lamb you can use it the next day in a shepherd's pie. I also love to fry the shredded pieces of meat in olive oil until really crispy and pile them into pittas or flatbreads with salad and tzatziki for a fast, easy and delicious dinner.

Fish en Papillote with Tomato and Olive Vinaigrette

En papillote is a French term for cooking food – usually fish – inside a paper parcel or a bag. It's a beautiful way to cook fish because it steams in the bag in its own juices and stays lovely and moist. If I'm preparing fish this way on the barbecue I use foil, but in the oven, baking parchment does the job. Served with a light but flavour-packed warm vinaigrette, this dish is a real winner.

SERVES: 4
PREP TIME: 15 MINUTES
COOKING TIME: ABOUT 20 MINUTES

4 tbsp olive oil

1 roasted red pepper from a jar, drained and finely chopped

1 red chilli, deseeded and thinly sliced

2 tbsp capers, drained

½ tsp herbes de Provence

4 fresh ripe tomatoes, diced

4 x 120–150g cod fillets, skin removed

1 large or 2 small lemons, thinly sliced

60g green and black pitted olives

sea salt and freshly ground black pepper

extra virgin olive oil, to finish

crusty bread, to serve

1. Heat the oil in a medium saucepan, then add the red pepper, chilli and a pinch of salt and pepper.

2. Add the capers and herbes de Provence, then stir for a minute to release the flavours. Tip in the tomatoes, stir through and simmer gently for 3–4 minutes while you cook the cod.

3. Preheat the oven to 180°C/160°C fan/gas 4 and put a baking tray inside to heat up.

4. Put one fillet of cod on a square of baking parchment, then add a drizzle of olive oil and some salt and pepper. Top with three slices of lemon. Wrap up the baking parchment to make a tightly sealed parcel. Repeat with the other three cod fillets.

5. Place the cod parcels on the hot baking tray and bake for 12–15 minutes.

6. Finely chop the olives and add to the sauce.

7. To serve, spoon the sauce onto four plates. Unwrap the parcels and place a cod fillet on top. Drizzle with a little extra virgin olive oil and serve with crusty bread.

Liver Lyonnaise

I love simple dishes like this when I'm cooking at home. Much like the Pommes Lyonnaise on page 78, Liver Lyonnaise comes from Lyon in the Rhône Valley towards the southeast of France and involves lots of luscious caramelised onions, which are spooned on top of pan-fried livers. This is great with a big pile of wilted greens for a warming winter meal or served with a crisp green salad and punchy vinaigrette in the summer.

SERVES: 4
PREP TIME: 10–15 MINUTES
COOKING TIME: 35–40 MINUTES

4 tbsp duck fat or olive oil, plus extra for the liver

3 large onions, sliced

1 bouquet garni (sprigs of thyme and parsley and bay leaves tied together)

2 garlic cloves, crushed

2 tsp caster sugar

100ml white wine

150ml good-quality chicken stock

4 x 100–125g slices of calf's liver, about ½–1cm thick

sea salt and freshly ground black pepper

chopped fresh flat-leaf parsley, to finish

1. Add the duck fat or olive oil to a sauté pan, add the onions, bouquet garni and salt and pepper and cook over low heat for 10 minutes, stirring frequently. Add the garlic, sugar and wine and cook for a few minutes. Pour in the stock, cover with a circle of baking parchment (cartouche) and continue cooking for another 15 minutes, or until softened and golden.

2. Remove the cartouche, increase the heat to medium and continue cooking the onions, stirring frequently so they don't catch, until they are caramelised and golden brown. This will take about 8–10 minutes. Remove the bouquet garni and set aside the onions while you prepare the liver.

3. Pat the liver slices dry with kitchen paper and season them with salt and pepper. Heat a dash of duck fat or olive oil in a frying pan over high heat, add half the liver and fry for 2–3 minutes, then turn over and fry for another 1–2 minutes on the other side. Remove from the pan and keep warm while you cook the remaining slices of liver.

4. To serve, place a slice of liver onto a serving plate and top with a generous spoonful of caramelised onions. Scatter with chopped parsley.

Braised Oxtail

This is the ultimate slow-cook dinner. Oxtail is a cut of meat with lots of connective tissue, so it needs a long, slow cook to break down and become tender. But while it may take some time, it's incredibly fuss free. Get all the ingredients into a casserole and leave the oven to work its magic while you get on with your day. It's delicious served with mashed potatoes – try it with my recipe for Pommes Mousseline on page 79.

SERVES: 4
PREP TIME: 30 MINUTES
COOKING TIME: ABOUT 5½ HOURS

1.5kg oxtail, sliced into 4cm chunks

1 whole garlic bulb, halved horizontally

2 tbsp olive oil, plus extra for drizzling

1 onion, roughly chopped

2 carrots, peeled and roughly chopped

2 celery sticks, roughly chopped

2 tbsp tomato purée

2 tbsp plain flour

500ml red wine

few sprigs of fresh rosemary

few sprigs of fresh thyme

2 bay leaves

750ml good-quality beef stock

1 x 400g tin chopped tomatoes

sea salt and freshly ground black pepper

chopped fresh parsley, to finish

creamy mashed potatoes or Pommes Mousseline (page 79) and greens, to serve

1. Preheat the oven to 220°C/200°C fan/gas 7.

2. Place the oxtail slices and halved garlic bulb in a roasting tray and season with salt and pepper and a drizzle of oil. Roast for 20 minutes, or until golden all over, then reduce the oven temperature to 160°C/140°C fan/gas 3.

3. Meanwhile, heat the oil in a large ovenproof casserole dish over medium heat. Add the onion, carrot and celery, season and fry for 10 minutes, or until softened. Add the tomato purée and fry for another couple of minutes, then add the flour and stir until it coats all the vegetables.

4. Add the roasted oxtail and garlic to the casserole dish, pour in the wine, add the herbs and cook over high heat until the liquid has reduced a little.

5. Pour in the stock and tinned tomatoes and stir. Bring to a very gentle simmer, cover and place in the oven for 4–5 hours, or until the meat is falling off the bone. Check it after a few hours and top up with more stock if it reduces too quickly.

6. Serve sprinkled with chopped parsley and mashed potatoes.

Pork Chops with Fennel, Sage and Onion

I have my mum to thank for this recipe; she used to make a version of this when I was a lad and the whole family would devour it. The classic French flavour combination of pork and fennel is enhanced with sage and onion and works an absolute treat. It also happens to be about as easy as it gets to cook, with very little preparation required and only a handful of ingredients. It makes a deliciously simple supper served with wilted cavolo nero or roasted Tenderstem broccoli.

SERVES: 4
PREP TIME: 15 MINUTES
COOKING TIME: ABOUT 1½ HOURS

1 tbsp olive oil

4 x 150–200g pork loin chops

1 large onion, thinly sliced

1 large fennel bulb, thinly sliced

½ bunch of fresh thyme

15 fresh sage leaves

2 tsp dried sage

50g cold butter, diced

sea salt and freshly ground black pepper

1. Preheat the oven to 180°C/160°C fan/gas 4.

2. Heat the oil in a frying pan over medium heat while you season the chops well with salt and pepper. Sear the chops on one side for 3 minutes (you may have to do this in two batches). Transfer the seared chops to a heavy ovenproof casserole or baking dish, unseared side down.

3. Cover the chops with the onion and fennel slices, separating the slices as you scatter them. The chops should be completely buried in the onions and fennel, so their juices will seep into the chops.

4. Top with the thyme sprigs, fresh and dried sage, and diced butter. Season well.

5. Cover the dish with a tight-fitting lid or seal with foil. Bake for about 1–1½ hours until the pork feels tender when pierced with the tip of a sharp knife. Two or three times during cooking, remove the lid or foil and tilt the dish so the juices run into one corner. Scoop up the juices and drizzle them over the chops, to baste them.

6. Serve the chops with the onions and fennel piled on top and the buttery juices spooned over and around.

Lamb Chops with Crispy Potatoes and Crème Fraîche

This is a lovely, simple supper that makes the most of the beautiful flavour that you get from lamb fat by rendering it and then saving it to fry the potatoes. Rendering is when fat is slowly warmed so that it melts without cooking the meat. This is also a great recipe for using up any leftover potatoes from another meal. I often cook more than I need so that I can have leftovers in the fridge for dishes just like this.

SERVES: 4
PREP TIME: 10 MINUTES
COOKING TIME: ABOUT 30 MINUTES

8 lamb chops

olive oil

750g baby new potatoes

2 sprigs of fresh rosemary, leaves chopped

1 tsp hot paprika

4 tbsp crème fraîche

sea salt and freshly ground black pepper

1. Heat a frying pan over low heat for 5 minutes. Add the chops, fat side down, to gently render the fat. Leave over low heat for 3–4 minutes until liquid fat appears in the pan. Transfer the lamb chops to a shallow bowl, drizzle with olive oil, salt and pepper and set aside. Reserve the lamb fat to fry the potatoes later.

2. Cook the new potatoes in a saucepan of boiling salted water for 15 minutes, or until tender when pierced with the tip of a knife. Drain and allow to cool slightly.

3. Transfer the chops to a new frying pan set over low-medium heat, or onto a barbecue grate. Cook for about 1–2 minutes on each side (depending on the thickness), allowing them to char in places. If using a barbecue, you can add a drizzle of olive oil on top of the chops to fan the flames and add an even smokier char. Remove the chops from the pan or grate and leave to rest for 5 minutes.

4. Meanwhile, slice the boiled potatoes and fry in the reserved lamb fat, seasoning as you go with most of the rosemary, salt and pepper. Add the paprika, and stir to combine.

5. To serve, pile the lamb chops onto plates with the crispy potatoes. Add a dollop of crème fraîche, then finish with a drizzle of olive oil and the rest of the chopped rosemary.

Madeleines

It makes me so happy that my daughter Jessie has caught the baking bug – these are exactly the sort of French treat that you'll find cooling on wire racks in our kitchen. You can vary the flavours of this simple sponge cake but I like to keep it classic and serve flavoured creams on the side. Most madeleine tins are 12-hole, so you'll need to bake a second batch to use up the mix. Photographed overleaf.

**MAKES: 16 LARGE MADELEINES
PREP TIME: 20 MINUTES, PLUS
20 MINUTES CHILLING
COOKING TIME: ABOUT 20 MINUTES,
PLUS COOLING**

2 eggs

100g caster sugar

grated zest of 1 lemon

100g plain flour, plus extra for
dusting

¾ tsp baking powder

100g butter, melted, plus extra for
greasing

icing sugar, to dust

FOR THE VANILLA CREAM
150ml whipping cream

1 tsp vanilla extract

2 tsp icing sugar

FOR THE RASPBERRY CREAM
150ml whipping cream

1 tsp vanilla extract

1 tbsp icing sugar

50g fresh raspberries, plus extra
to serve

1. In a medium mixing bowl, whisk the eggs and sugar together with an electric whisk for 3–5 minutes until fluffy and the beaters leave a trail or 'ribbon' on the surface of the batter when lifted (this is called the ribbon stage). Add the lemon zest and mix again, just enough to combine.

2. In a separate bowl, mix the flour and baking powder together, then sift this mixture over the batter and carefully fold this in. Add the melted butter and mix gently until a smooth batter is formed.

3. Cover the madeleine batter with clingfilm and chill in the fridge for 20 minutes. Preheat the oven to 200°C/180°C fan/gas 6.

4. Using a pastry brush, grease a 12-hole madeleine tin with melted butter. Shake a little flour on top, to coat, tapping out the excess.

5. Divide the mix evenly among the holes of the madeleine tin (don't fill each one more than three-quarters full). Bake for 8–10 minutes until lightly golden and firm to the touch.

6. Release the madeleines from the tin as soon as you remove it from the oven – so they do not stick – and cool them on a wire rack. Bake the leftover mix in the same way.

7. Make the flavoured creams. For the vanilla cream, place the whipping cream into a bowl, add the vanilla extract and icing sugar and whisk with an electric whisk until it forms soft peaks. Spoon into a serving bowl. For the raspberry cream, pour the whipping cream into a bowl, add the vanilla extract and icing sugar. Place the raspberries into a sieve and press through the sieve over the cream to extract the juice and remove the seeds. Whisk this mixture together with an electric whisk until it forms soft peaks and then spoon into a serving bowl.

8. Dust the madeleines with icing sugar and serve with the vanilla and raspberry cream to dip into. These are best on the same day they're made.

Banana Split Crêpes

Who doesn't love a good pancake, especially French-style, thin and crispy crêpes? And these are even better with a retro banana split twist. Crêpes are the perfect recipe to get your kids in the kitchen with you; the batter is simple to make and they'll love helping you swirl it around the pan! I can't be sure that the French would approve of this mash-up, but I guarantee your family will.

SERVES: 4
PREP TIME: 20 MINUTES
COOKING TIME: ABOUT 15 MINUTES

130g plain flour

300ml milk

2 eggs

150ml double cream, whipped

1 tbsp olive oil or melted butter

2 bananas, peeled, sliced

FOR THE HOT NUTELLA SAUCE
4 tbsp Nutella

2 tsp cocoa powder

6 tbsp milk

4 tbsp chopped toasted hazelnuts
(approx. 30g)

1. To make the crêpe batter, add the flour to a mixing bowl and make a well in the centre. Whisk the milk and eggs together, then gradually add this mixture to the flour until it forms a smooth batter. Transfer the batter to a jug and allow the mix to rest.

2. Softly whip the cream and set aside.

3. To make the hot Nutella sauce, put the Nutella, cocoa powder and milk into a saucepan. Place over low heat and bring to a gentle simmer, whisking. Simmer for 5 minutes, stirring often, until thick. Keep warm.

4. To cook the crêpes, brush a large non-stick frying pan with olive oil or butter using a pastry brush. Place over medium heat; when hot, add a little of the mix from the jug and tilt the pan to distribute it evenly and create a thin crêpe. When lightly browned, and the top is no longer sticky to touch, gently fold the crêpe in half, then in half again and remove from the pan to a warm plate. Repeat until the mix is all used – you should have 8 thin crêpes.

5. Bring the Nutella sauce back to a simmer then add half the hazelnuts and remove from the heat.

6. Serve 2 warm crêpes per person, with sliced bananas, a good dollop of whipped cream, the hot Nutella sauce and the remaining hazelnuts.

Giant Rum Baba

Baba au rhum are traditionally small, individual cakes, but I wanted to create a giant version of this classic French recipe for extra wow factor. The cake itself is made with a yeast-risen dough and is fairly dry, but it comes to life when it's been soaked in a sticky, sweet, boozy syrup. I love to serve it with mascarpone whipped cream. You will need a bundt tin approx. 24cm in diameter and 10cm deep.

SERVES: 10–12
PREP TIME: 30 MINUTES, PLUS 1½ HOURS RESTING
COOKING TIME: 30–35 MINUTES

150ml warm water

2 tbsp caster sugar

8g dried active yeast (not instant, fast-action or easy bake)

150g butter, plus extra for greasing

400g strong white bread flour, plus extra for dusting

1 tsp table salt

4 eggs, beaten

cocoa powder, for dusting

FOR THE SYRUP
200g golden caster sugar

1 vanilla pod, split lengthways and seeds scraped out

100ml white rum

FOR THE WHIPPED MASCARPONE
100ml double cream

100g crème fraîche

100g mascarpone

1. In a jug, mix together the warm water and a pinch of the sugar, then sprinkle over the dried yeast and stir to activate it. Leave for 5 minutes in a warm place, or until it is frothy on top.

2. Meanwhile, melt the butter in a saucepan over gentle heat, then set aside.

3. Put the flour, salt and remaining sugar into a large bowl and mix together. Make a well in the centre of the flour and pour in the yeasty liquid. Stir together and add the beaten egg a little at a time until it is all incorporated. Finally stir in the melted butter and mix until you have a smooth batter.

4. Use a piece of kitchen paper to grease your bundt tin with a little butter. Pour the batter into the greased tin, then tap the tray on your work surface until the dough has flattened. Cover the tin with a piece of lightly greased clingfilm and allow the dough to rise at room temperature for 1–1½ hours, or until it reaches the top of the tin.

5. Preheat the oven to 180°C/160°C fan/gas 4.

6. Once the dough has fully risen, remove the clingfilm, place the bundt tin in the oven and bake for 30–35 minutes until evenly golden brown. Remove from the oven and allow to cool for 10–15 minutes in the bundt tin.

7. While the baba is baking, make the syrup. Put the sugar and vanilla (seeds and pod) into a large saucepan and cover with 200ml of water. Place over medium heat and slowly bring to the boil until all the sugar has dissolved and it has turned syrupy – this should take 6–8 minutes. Remove from the heat and add the white rum. Allow to cool until lukewarm. Once the syrup has cooled a little but is still warm, place the baba in a serving dish and pour the syrup slowly over the top and leave to steep in the syrup.

8. To make the whipped mascarpone, combine all the ingredients in a bowl and mix until thickened (it should be thick enough to hold its shape when spooned onto the baba).

9. To serve, slice the baba into thick wedges. Spoon over a dollop of the whipped mascarpone and lightly dust with a little cocoa powder. Pour the excess syrup over the baba if you wish.

MARCUS'S TIP

Vanilla pods are expensive – they can and should be used more than once. Even if the seeds have been removed you can still use the pod – simply remove it from the cooled syrup and either dry it out and retain for future use or pop it into some caster sugar to create vanilla sugar.

Cherry Clafoutis

This is an absolute corker of a French dessert: thick batter is poured over fruit and baked until puffed up and golden brown, almost like a sweet version of a Yorkshire pudding. I've used cherries, which are the traditional fruit for a clafoutis, but almost any other fruit works with this recipe; I've had apricot, peach and even apple before when I've eaten it in France. It's also a great one for using tinned fruit, which would make it more economical too.

SERVES: 4
PREP TIME: 15 MINUTES
COOKING TIME: ABOUT 55 MINUTES

50g butter, plus extra for greasing

2 tbsp caster sugar

4 tbsp Demerara sugar

400g fresh black cherries, stones removed (pitted weight approx. 360g)

150ml double cream

150ml milk

seeds from 1 vanilla pod

grated zest of 1 lemon

2 eggs

45g caster sugar

45g plain flour

1 tbsp icing sugar, for dusting

FOR THE LAVENDER CREAM

200ml whipping or double cream

1 tsp edible lavender flowers

1 tsp vanilla extract

1 tbsp icing sugar

1. Lightly grease a round metal skillet or ceramic dish, approx. 23cm in diameter, with butter and sprinkle with caster sugar (this will help the clafoutis to rise). Preheat the oven to 180°C/160°C fan/gas 4 and place a baking sheet into the oven to heat up.

2. Put the Demerara sugar with 2 tablespoons of water into a small heavy-based saucepan or frying pan. Place over medium heat and leave to melt and caramelise to a deep golden colour, swirling the pan occasionally (do not stir) to get an even colour – this will take 5–8 minutes. Add the butter, whisk well and simmer for 1–2 minutes until well combined.

3. Pour the caramel into the prepared dish then quickly, while the caramel is still hot, add the cherries in an even layer on top of the caramel.

4. Put the cream, milk, vanilla seeds and lemon zest into a small saucepan and gently bring to the boil. Remove from the heat.

5. In a deep bowl, whisk together the eggs and caster sugar. Whisk in the flour, then gradually add the hot milk and cream, whisking continuously. Pour this batter over the cherries, then place the dish into the oven onto the hot baking sheet. Bake for about 45 minutes, or until golden, puffed up and cooked through.

6. While the clafoutis is cooking, make the lavender cream. Place the cream into a saucepan, add the lavender flowers and heat over low heat until it just starts bubbling at the sides of the pan. Remove from the heat before it starts simmering and set aside to cool. Once cool, strain the cream through a sieve and discard the lavender. Add the vanilla extract and icing sugar and whisk until it forms soft peaks. Spoon into a serving bowl.

7. Remove the clafoutis from the oven, dust with icing sugar and serve immediately with the lavender cream alongside.

Apricot Trifle with Elderflower, White Wine and Lavender Jelly

I adore a trifle and really wanted to create one inspired by some of my favourite French flavours: lavender, elderflower liqueur and apricots. Trifle always brings a smile to people's faces when you present it for dessert. You will need an 8–12cm trifle dish.

SERVES: 8–10
PREP TIME: ABOUT 45 MINUTES,
PLUS 2½ HOURS CHILLING
COOKING TIME: 10 MINUTES

**FOR THE WHITE WINE
AND LAVENDER JELLY**
750ml dry white wine
115g caster sugar
75ml elderflower liqueur (or elderflower cordial)
2 tbsp edible lavender flowers
6 sheets of gelatine

FOR THE SPONGE LAYER
12 trifle sponge fingers (80g)
2 tbsp elderflower liqueur (or elderflower cordial)

FOR THE FRUIT LAYER
2 x 400g tins apricot halves in juice, drained

FOR THE ELDERFLOWER CREAM
400ml double cream
seeds from 1 vanilla pod
2 tbsp icing sugar, sifted
100g crème fraîche
2 tbsp elderflower liqueur (or elderflower cordial)

TO DECORATE
1 tsp edible lavender flowers, crushed
30g pistachio nuts, roughly chopped
grated orange zest

1. Start by making the jelly. Heat the white wine, sugar, elderflower liqueur, 50ml of cold water and the lavender flowers in a saucepan and reduce over medium heat for 8–10 minutes until the sugar has dissolved and the flavour has intensified. Remove from the heat and allow to infuse and cool slightly. Strain through a fine sieve into a large jug and discard the lavender flowers.

2. Soak the gelatine sheets in a bowl of cold water for 3–5 minutes. Squeeze the soaked gelatine sheets to remove the water and stir into the wine mixture until dissolved. Allow to cool to room temperature.

3. Arrange the sponge fingers in the base of a trifle dish. Drizzle with the 2 tablespoons of elderflower liqueur, then pour a little of the jelly over the sponge, to just cover. Chill in the fridge for 30 minutes, or until firm enough to set the sponge in the base. Once it's set, pour the remaining jelly over the top and return to the fridge for 2 hours.

4. Once the jelly has fully set, remove from the fridge. Slice each apricot half into four slices, then arrange these over the top of the jelly.

5. To make the cream, put the double cream, vanilla seeds and icing sugar into a large bowl and use an electric whisk to whip the cream to soft peaks. Fold in the crème fraîche and elderflower liqueur to combine.

6. Spoon the cream over the fruit and swirl the top to create peaks. Scatter with the crushed lavender flowers, chopped pistachio nuts and finish with a little orange zest.

MARCUS'S TIP

I have controversially left the custard layer out of this one, but you are very welcome to add one if you can't live without it!

Conversion Chart

DRY WEIGHTS

METRIC	IMPERIAL
5g	¼oz
8/10g	⅓oz
15g	½oz
20g	¾oz
25g	1oz
30/35g	1¼oz
40g	1½oz
50g	2oz
60/70g	2½oz
75/85/90g	3oz
100g	3½oz
110/120g	4oz
125/130g	4½oz
135/140/150g	5oz
170/175g	6oz
200g	7oz
225g	8oz
250g	9oz
265g	9½oz
275g	10oz
300g	11oz
325g	11½oz
350g	12oz
375g	13oz

METRIC	IMPERIAL
400g	14oz
425g	15oz
450g	1lb
475g	1lb 1oz
500g	1lb 2oz
550g	1lb 3oz
600g	1lb 5oz
625g	1lb 6oz
650g	1lb 7oz
675g	1½lb
700g	1lb 9oz
750g	1lb 10oz
800g	1¾lb
850g	1lb 14oz
900g	2lb
950g	2lb 2oz
1kg	2lb 3oz
1.1kg	2lb 6oz
1.25kg	2¾lb
1.3/1.4kg	3lb
1.5kg	3lb 5oz
1.75/1.8kg	4lb
2kg	4lb 4oz

LIQUID MEASURES

METRIC	IMPERIAL (US)	CUPS
15ml	½fl oz	1 tbsp
20ml	¾fl oz	
30ml	1fl oz	⅛ cup
60ml	2fl oz	¼ cup
75ml	2½fl oz	
90ml	3fl oz	⅓ cup
100ml	3½fl oz	
120ml	4fl oz	½ cup
135ml	4½fl oz	
160ml	5fl oz	⅔ cup
180ml	6fl oz	¾ cup
210ml	7fl oz	
240ml	8fl oz	1 cup
265ml	9fl oz	
300ml	10fl oz	1¼ cups
350ml	12fl oz	1½ cups
415ml	14fl oz	
480ml	16fl oz / 1 pint	2 cups
530ml	18fl oz	2¼ cups
1 litre	32fl oz	4 cups

OVEN TEMPERATURES

°C	°F	GAS MARK	DESCRIPTION
110	225	¼	cool
120	250	½	cool
140	275	1	very low
150	300	2	very low
160	325	3	low to moderate
170/180	350	4	moderate
190	375	5	moderately hot
200	400	6	hot
210/220	425	7	hot
230/240	450	8	hot

Index

F

G

H

Sauce 31

see also smoked haddock

hake

Bouillabaisse-inspired Fish Soup 208, *209*

ham

Cassoulet 192, *193*

Creamy Mussels with Pastis and Bayonne Ham *140*, 141

haricot beans

Cassoulet 192, *193*

Provençal Beans 113

hazelnuts

Honeyed Carrots with Crème Fraîche and Hazelnuts 98, *99*

Nutella Sauce 222

Salad 171

White Fish with Hazelnut Crumb and Hollandaise Sauce 31

Herb Dressing 110

Herbed Garlic Butter *32*, 33

Herby Green Sauce 108

Hollandaise Sauce 31

Omelette Arnold Bennett 57

Honeyed Carrots with Crème Fraîche and Hazelnuts 98, *99*

I

Icing 152–3

ingredients 12

J

jelly

Apricot Trifle with Elderflower, White Wine and

Lavender Jelly 228, *229*

Jerusalem artichokes

Mushroom and Jerusalem Artichoke Velouté 142, *143*

juniper berries

Torte de Gibier with Madeira and Truffle Sauce 73–4, *75*

K

kale

Bulgar Wheat Salad with Roasted Kale and Butternut Squash *206*, 207

Koffman, Pierre 11, 14

Kromberg, Peter 14

L

Ladenis, Nico 14

lamb

Lamb Chops with Crispy Potatoes and Crème Fraîche 218

Lamb Chops with Roast Pumpkin, Black Olive and Anchovy 183, *184*

Lamb Ribs with Sweet Calvados Glaze 112

Slow Roast Leg of Lamb with Mint and Caper Sauce 210–11

lamb's lettuce

Salad 171

lavender

Apricot Trifle with Elderflower, White Wine and Lavender Jelly 228, *229*

Churros with Lavender Sugar and Citrus Cream 47–8, *49*

Lavender Cream 226

M

N

S

U

V

W

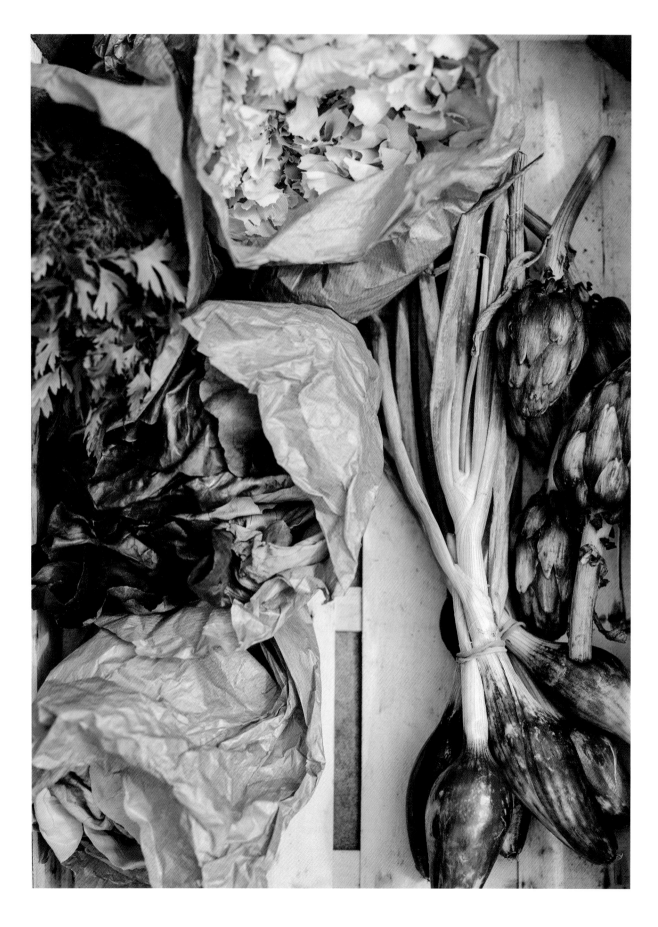

Acknowledgements

It's been an absolute pleasure writing this book; having the opportunity to look back over my career has been a real privilege. I hope you enjoy cooking these recipes as much as I have enjoyed bringing them all together. This my tenth cookbook now and, as always, I couldn't have done it alone.

My incomparable publisher, Katya Shipster, has once again steered me through this process and drawn a book out of me that I am extremely proud of. Thank you always for your support and guidance. Project Editor Sarah Hammond is absolute dynamite – thank you for bringing the team together and quite literally making it all happen. Thank you to the best designer in the business, Sim Greenaway, whose vision for this book has resulted in something really special. And to the rest of the team at HarperCollins in sales, marketing and publicity: Natasha Photiou, Orlando Mowbray and Tom Hill, it takes a village and I'm very grateful that you're in mine.

A huge thank you goes to our photographer, Matt Russell, who brought the recipes to life so perfectly, alongside prop stylist Rachel Vere, both of whom have an incredible eye for detail and have made the food look as beautiful as it is delicious. Speaking of delicious, my thanks also go to the dream team of food stylists – Lisa Harrison, Anna Burges-Lumsden and Ellie Mulligan – who made each of the dishes in this book look and taste extraordinary.

When it comes to generating 90 recipes that not only have to taste good, but be exciting, inspiring and easy to achieve at home – especially while juggling a busy *MasterChef* filming schedule – you need a trusted side kick and I'm lucky enough to have the best in Lisa Harrison. Thank you for everything you've put into this book, I hope you're as proud of it as I am. Thanks also to testers and developers Anna Burges-Lumsden, Alice Hughes and Isla Murray for all your help. Huge thanks also to the indispensable Clare Sayer, copy editor extraordinaire.

Thank you to the newly hitched Bridget Powell, we have worked together on many TV projects, and it turns out you have another brilliant hidden talent; it has been a great pleasure to have you working on this book as my co-author. You just understand me and what I am trying to say, and you manage to put that into words so that others can understand at speed whilst always remaining calm. A massive heartfelt thank you to you. What's next?

To my agent M&C Saatchi Merlin – Richard Thompson, Nicola Wright and the rest of the team, who do the most amazing job of looking after me, thank you for your unwavering support, I am so lucky to have you by my side.

And finally to Jane, Jake, Archie and Jessie, thank you for being my biggest and most honest fans. Love you.

HarperCollinsPublishers
1 London Bridge Street
London SE1 9GF

www.harpercollins.co.uk

HarperCollinsPublishers
Macken House, 39/40 Mayor Street Upper
Dublin 1, D01 C9W8, Ireland

First published by *HarperCollinsPublishers* 2024

10 9 8 7 6 5 4 3 2 1

Text © Marcus Wareing 2024
Photography © Matt Russell 2024

Marcus Wareing asserts the moral right to be identified as the author of this work

A catalogue record of this book is available from the British Library

ISBN 978-0-00-871412-3

Food Styling: Lisa Harrison, Anna Burges-Lumsden, Ellie Mulligan
Prop Styling: Rachel Vere

Printed and bound by GPS in Bosnia & Herzegovina

MIX
Paper | Supporting
responsible forestry
FSC™ C007454

This book is produced from FSC™ certified paper and other controlled sources to ensure responsible forest management.

For more information visit: www.harpercollins.co.uk/green

WHEN USING KITCHEN APPLIANCES PLEASE ALWAYS FOLLOW THE MANUFACTURER'S INSTRUCTIONS